The Power of Experience

Principals Talk about School Improvement

Linda K. Wagner

With the assistance of Cheryl Brumbaugh-Cayford

ROWMAN & LITTLEFIELD EDUCATION
A division of
ROWMAN & LITTLEFIELD PUBLISHERS, INC.
Lanham • New York • Toronto • Plymouth, UK

Published by Rowman & Littlefield Education
A division of Rowman & Littlefield Publishers, Inc.
A wholly owned subsidary of The Rowman & Littlefield Publishing Group, Inc.
4501 Forbes Boulevard, Suite 200, Lanham, Maryland 20706
www.rowman.com

10 Thornbury Road, Plymouth PL6 7PP, United Kingdom

British Library Cataloguing in Publication Information Available

Library of Congress Cataloging-in-Publication Data

Wagner, Linda K., 1965–
The power of experience : principals talk about school improvement / Linda K. Wagner, with the
assistance of Cheryl Brumbaugh-Cayford.
p. cm.
ISBN 978-1-4758-0018-0 (pbk. : alk. paper) — ISBN 978-1-4758-0019-7 (electronic)
1. School improvement programs—United States. 2. School principals—United States. 3. School
management and organization—United States. 4. School supervision—United States. I. Title.
LB2822.82.W34 2012
371.2'07—dc23
2012029209

™
The paper used in this publication meets the minimum requirements of American
National Standard for Information Sciences Permanence of Paper for Printed Library
Materials, ANSI/NISO Z39.48-1992.

Printed in the United States of America

This book is dedicated to my parents, who helped me imagine what is possible through hard work and an optimistic spirit.

Contents

Acknowledgments

Special thanks to Theresa Brunn, Jason Buchanan, Jason Cameron, Dr. Deborah Collins, Dr. Dennis Fox, Dr. Jack Gyves, Elizabeth Heiny, Sarah Heiny, Nadia Hillman, Cynthia Lathrop, Kristin Mariconda, Stuart Payne, Dr. Frank Rodriguez, Dr. Julie Vitale, Dr. Cheri Warren, Rebecca Wetzel, and Connie Wu.

The author also gratefully acknowledges the invaluable assistance of Cheryl Brumbaugh-Cayford in compiling and organizing the material for this book. Without her aid, this project would never have been completed.

Introduction

The Power of Experience: Principals Talk about School Improvement is a guide for principals, both aspiring and established, who hope to make a measurable difference in the achievement of all students, and who strive to create a positive, safe, and student-centered learning environment in their schools.

School and district administrators often find themselves searching for mentors to help them to become effective instructional leaders. Several nationwide organizations acknowledged the need for principal guidance in the area of school improvement, and agreed to contribute their expertise to this work. At the suggestion of the American Association of School Administrators (AASA) and with the support of the National Association of Elementary School Principals (NAESP), a network of over fifty exemplary and award-winning principals were interviewed. This generous sharing of advice and wisdom of principals with academic expertise was culled and synthesized to become the core content of this book.

This content was gleaned from interviews with principals who have been instrumental in having their schools designated as U.S. Department of Education National Blue Ribbon Schools, or who were identified as National Distinguished Principals by the National Association of Elementary School Principals. The book draws on the wisdom and experience of school leaders from across the nation and in select locations around the world. From Kenya to California, Alaska to Wisconsin, these principals reflect great diversity but oneness of purpose: reaching and teaching all children by building exceptional schools through exemplary leadership. Whether new to the field or a veteran principal, you will benefit from the collective wisdom, insight, and experience of principals who have built remarkable schools designed to promote student achievement.

This book will help principals assess where their schools stand on the continuum leading toward school improvement, and understand the elements necessary to build a school culture around high expectations of continuous academic improvement. Readers will obtain the tools they need to challenge the status quo. They will learn to make meaningful school-wide changes that help students learn and achieve. In this book, principals learn to create a climate of focused, skilled, and motivated teachers working in a cohesive school environment in which teaching and learning are of the highest importance.

ORGANIZATION OF THE BOOK

The Power of Experience: Principals Talk about School Improvement is divided into ten chapters. Chapter 1 begins by defining and exploring what it means to be an effective principal. Chapters 2 and 3 examine a principal's role in the instructional improvement process, exploring the importance of building a culture of continuous improvement designed to improve student success. Chapter 4 focuses on assessment and accountability. Chapter 5 discusses the hiring, training, and retention of personnel. Chapter 6 highlights ways to create effective site-based management. Chapter 7 provides ways to enhance parent participation in schools. Chapter 8 outlines ways principals can work effectively with the central office. Chapter 9 addresses how best to manage and balance the demands of a principal's professional and personal time. The final chapter presents some great ideas from the principals who took part in this study.

An appendix offers checklists, sample letters, and tools designed to assist principals and aspiring principals in implementing the improvement efforts outlined in the book. Following the appendix is a list of books recommended by study participants.

ONE

Characteristics of Effective Principals

Principals need actionable steps that they can take to build a culture of continuous improvement in their schools, with student achievement at its core. This book provides those steps from the personal and professional experience of fifty study participants who have earned recognition as either National Distinguished Principals or National Blue Ribbon School Principals. The principals or prospective principals who master these learnable leadership skills can anticipate greater success in their efforts to build student achievement and enhance overall school improvement.

Throughout our study, we found that principals who are passionate about meeting student needs tend to have characteristics that promote effective instructional leadership. These characteristics are:

- *Passion*: These principals are focused, goal oriented, and have high expectations.
- *Integrity*: They are honest, trustworthy, and set a good example for others.
- *Communication skills*: They convey messages clearly and effectively.
- *Knowledge of curriculum and instruction*: They are well versed in methods designed to create effective teaching and learning.

PASSION

Passionate principals have energy and commitment for their work, making student learning one of their highest priorities. Although student instruction does not come to principals as an urgent issue to be handled immediately, effective school leaders give it precedence, putting quality instruction at the forefront of their efforts to build a successful school.

> *We like to say, "Everything you do is a self portrait. Autograph all your work with excellence."*
> — Author unknown; quoted by Andrew M. Doell, National Blue Ribbon School Principal, New York

Effective principals lead steadily in the direction of instructional improvement. They build systems of interventions designed to close achievement gaps and assist those students most in need of help. They are persistent in their efforts to examine data. They work tirelessly with teachers to identify which students are and are not successfully mastering the content delivered in class, seeking ways to help teachers meet the needs of harder-to-reach students. They are willing to provide an uneven set of resources to students who struggle, in order to give underperforming students a greater chance to succeed. These principals understand that "closing the achievement gap" means that students who need the greatest instructional resources and the most help must secure the attention of skilled teachers and the books, materials, and curricular resources they need in order to be successful.

Effective instructional leaders spend time determining what areas of focus are most important for their schools, and they help staff decide not only what to do but also what not to do if the school team hopes to focus on instructional change and improvement.

Principals with passion for instruction imagine an optimistic future for their schools. They understand the impact of their decisions, and use their influence to build cultures of continuous academic improvement in the schools they lead.

> *Good, better, best. Never let it rest until your good is better and your better is best.*
>
> —St. Jerome

Principals who get results for the students they serve are unwavering in their high expectations. While approaching the work with understanding and kindness, principals who are instructional leaders continuously encourage others to work toward commonly held goals. Effective principals maintain a firm belief that the team can build a culture of continuous improvement with student achievement at its core.

Principals may pause to reframe their work, but over the course of time, the trajectory of their work leads to overall school improvement. Effective principals know that day by day, step by step, the adults delivering instructional services to students must become better at the work of building student achievement, guided by strong principal leadership.

> *I set high expectations for myself and others in the building, and I don't waver from those expectations.*
> —Kelly Wilmore, National Blue Ribbon School Principal, Virginia

Excellent principals make it a point to be visible by personally supervising students, interacting with parents, and visiting every classroom frequently. Because principals accomplish their most important work in cooperation with others, their visibility and relationships with others throughout the school system are vital to student success. These principals spend school hours with constituents, completing paperwork in the evening or after most of their staff and students have left for the day.

INTEGRITY

Integrity is one of the core leadership qualities that make effective principals positive and productive leaders. People trust them because leaders with integrity do what they say they will do. They gain the trust of constituents by following through on promises. If they cannot complete a task, they do not volunteer for it. Promised tasks get done, and they are done on time.

> *Walk your talk. Do what you say, and you say what you do. Building trust is a matter of character and competence. If you don't have both, you can't build trust.*
> —Budd Dingwall, National Distinguished Principal, North Carolina

Honest leaders provide access to information that can be shared. They keep their staff members informed of changes affecting the school, ensuring that documents such as budgets, policies, updates, and other relevant school information is available to those who are interested in such documents. Effective principals may even go out of their way to post these documents in public areas so that people have easy access to school information.

Trust in the leader is built, at least in part, when constituents sense information is being shared with them openly and honestly.

Anybody looking at me in my role as principal would see that I am very transparent. People know what I am thinking. I involve lots of people. They can see inside what's going on. Things don't come by surprise. I involve, I communicate, and I make sure people know my thinking. . . . I involve the stakeholders. The buy-in has been tremendous.
                    —Brian M. Hull, National Distinguished Principal, Virginia

Effective principals know how to set staff members in motion toward a desired goal or objective, supporting them with the tools and resources they need, demonstrating confidence that employees will do their jobs with competence and professionalism, and then getting out of the way.

Instead of a top-down leadership, I trust my staff to come up with decisions and ideas that will better our school. I don't always agree with some of the decisions, but have found that things have worked out in almost all situations. . . . I do have the power to override their suggestions but rarely do I do it, because of past success. The more brains that are working on a topic or solution, the better the decision will be. I have also found that staff will buy into a program or idea a lot better if it comes from them.
                    —Wayne C. Roellich, National Blue Ribbon School Principal,
                                                                    Washington

Listening is central to the role of the principal. Spending time with teachers who face a dilemma, or helping and encouraging them when they are struggling, is key to the principal's job. In the role of listener, a principal may encourage a teacher to seek professional development opportunities or brainstorm with a teacher about ideas to help a child with specific needs. The principal's availability to act as a sounding board for teacher struggles, questions, and concerns is critical to problem solving at the school.

When the team member feels understood, he or she begins to feel that the principal is in a position to help, or at least to understand the situation. Empathy is a relationship builder. While the principal cannot and should not always fix difficult situations, the use of empathetic listening can help the principal understand the plight of a teacher who has had a particularly difficult day, month, or year. This practice builds in the school staff a sense that the principal understands their problems and difficulties. Effective principals see themselves as the person central to understanding and ensuring that teachers have what they need to reach every child, every day.

"Being known and valued" goes for the adults in the building as well as the students. We trust one another on a fundamental, emotional level, and are becoming more open to acknowledging our weaknesses. I appreciate that all of the adults in the school have unique stories, are burdened by personal sadness, and strengthened by their family, friends, and colleagues in ways that impact the learning community. Without recognizing this, we cannot be passionate, committed, accountable, or attentive to ourselves and our students.

By attending to the morale and noticing the culture of the building, I ensure that when it comes time to focus on the "nitty gritty" of our professional work and high expectations, we as teachers can have the critical and status quo–challenging conversations that can lead to improved teacher and student performance. This is not easy to do, and indeed can become "messy" if relationships haven't been nurtured and genuine personal connections haven't been established.

—Dr. Christopher Kennedy, National Distinguished Principal,
Rhode Island

COMMUNICATION SKILLS

Principals who hope to be instructional leaders spend time studying techniques of effective communication, including public speaking, active listening, and having difficult or courageous conversations. Because they improve instruction through guiding and supervising the work of teachers in classrooms, as principals continuously communicate they also continuously work toward the desired change essential to the improvement process.

Everything you choose to do or not to do sends a message. If you see a piece of trash in the hall and you pick it up, you've sent a message. If you take a call with concern, or don't take the call at all, that sends a message. The way you dress, the questions you ask, give others a glimpse of your values and your beliefs. People are watching and listening. You have impact. If you are not consistent, they will not buy in.

—Andrew M. Doell, National Blue Ribbon School Principal, New York

One of the most important aspects of effective leadership is setting a good example. When the leader, with a spirit of humility, does the work he or she is asking of others, the team quickly comes to view the leader as one willing to serve as well as lead. This may mean climbing on to the school roof to retrieve balls after the kickball game or flipping pancakes for the pancake breakfast. These tasks would not normally fall within the domain of the principal. But service-oriented leadership creates loyalty among staff members, who are more likely to pitch in for the common good if their principal does the same.

> *If I'm asking someone to do something, I should be able and willing to do it myself. They need to know I'm a team player. There have been times when I've picked up a mop if needed. I'll help in the office, or cover in the classroom. I don't ask of others what I'm not willing to do myself.*
> —Brian Hull, National Distinguished Principal, Virginia

The principal promotes the mission, culture, and positive instructional orientation of the school through the principal's actions and interactions. From the way the principal behaves in the community to the way he or she talks to a kindergartener, people are watching the message that is sent. Effective principals ensure that the messages they send are positive and focused on what is best for students.

KNOWLEDGE OF CURRICULUM AND INSTRUCTION

Principals should be knowledgeable about the curriculum offered at the school. They should be attuned to the expectations for students at each grade level. They should be up to date on current instructional research findings. They should know the strategies that lead to teacher effectiveness.

Such leaders should not only be cognizant of the latest techniques in teaching and learning, but, if asked to step into a classroom to demonstrate these skills, they should also be ready and willing to do so with enthusiasm and competence.

In order to achieve a high level of knowledge in the areas of curriculum and instruction, effective principals spend time studying best practices in teaching and learning. They read educational research and share the information with their staff. They conduct model lessons to train and assist teachers.

Whether teaching children or adults, effective principals are energetic participants in the process of school improvement through research, teaching, and training. This ensures that they remain knowledgeable and at the forefront of educational research and instructional delivery.

A STORY FROM THE FIELD

Told by Jill Flanders, National Distinguished Principal, Massachusetts

We had three young children who came to preschool with complicated diag-noses for autism. The practice had been to send them out for an outside place-ment. I was working with a visionary special education director and another staff member. We wanted to keep them at our school and take them on as a challenge.

We decided to invent a program. We worked with their parents and created a preschool for autistic children. We made some pretty big mistakes up front. The families were understanding and patient. We were doing pretty intensive training with the people we hired to work with these students. We had an autism specialist come in and work with the teachers. We equipped a room.

We started by keeping the autistic students separate from the other stu-dents, and then we said, "What were we thinking?" Integrating them into other classes was another layer of training we needed to do.

Those children are still in this district. They have friends at their own grade level. Their parents are marvelous advocates. That, to me, is the biggest success story we've had here.

There were "going home in tears" days when we knew we had missed a step and we didn't know what else we could do. There were weeks when we had made tremendous gains — and then they would come back in a week and it was like they had never learned in the first place. But we kept at it and have been successful.

TWO

Guiding Improvements in Teaching and Learning

INSTRUCTIONAL LEADERSHIP PROMOTES ACHIEVEMENT

Schools are expected to constantly change and evolve. Pressures from the state, federal, and local levels, educational research, and common sense tell educators that they must alter instruction frequently to meet the rapidly evolving needs of the students they serve.

But how much change is enough? How much is too much? And how can a principal control the rate and pace of school-wide improvements? Doubtless you have heard or asked these questions about your school.

A school is like a tall and stately mountain. It may look strong, and it may stand out in the community in important ways. But change, even if we cannot see it from day to day, is inevitable. A mountain can be built up through seismic or volcanic activity, but if it is not being built up, chances are it is eroding. Pebbles fall here, water removes a layer of soil there, and over time the topography alters.

Just like nature's topography, learning systems are rarely in a steady state. Every day, at every school, teaching is improving through efforts to create positive change, or it is stagnating, or it is in decline. Instructional erosion may occur. Each day there are incremental changes in a school that are relatively invisible. Over time, however, these changes can stealthily but completely transform the landscape.

For better or worse, the world is a dynamic place and change happens. While we cannot control much of what happens in the wider world around us, principals do have a significant influence on how transformation occurs in their school and what kind of transformation that may be.

What is measured in a school often may be what gets done, or what is considered to be accomplished. It also is true that what is not measured or observed may not get the attention it deserves. Systems that are languishing or weakening often are by-products of a pervasive inattention to critical factors, or perhaps a lack of focused effort on improvement.

Quality instruction in all classrooms is of critical importance to school-wide instructional excellence. Each instructor's attention to excellence and detail is essential. Sometimes, however, effectiveness erodes due to shortcuts, inattention, or a lack of effort.

One day, for example, a teacher may discover he or she can get by without writing lesson plans. Each day thereafter, the validity of that discovery may be reinforced because it is easier not to put plans in writing than it is to commit them to paper. After all, the teacher may be thinking, the classroom still appears to be functioning. Even the teacher may not notice the decline in preparation, although lack of adequate planning will doubtlessly manifest itself over time. Inevitably the teacher's instructional effectiveness erodes. Without frequent checks from the principal, the teacher may stop writing plans altogether.

If this type of instructional erosion is allowed to continue, habits of this type will have a dramatic impact on student success. If such erosion happens in more than one classroom, it will have a negative effect on school-wide academic results.

Even if instruction in a school is solid and of high quality, new strategies and techniques, standards for learning, and advancements will require constant change and improvement. Active growth and transformation is necessary in all classrooms in order to create a school-wide culture of continuous improvement—with student achievement at its core.

THE PRINCIPAL'S ROLE IN GUIDING SCHOOL-WIDE IMPROVEMENT

A principal's presence in classrooms plays a key role in school-wide instructional change and improvement. If there is little administrative presence in classrooms or guidance at the school-wide level, teachers essentially become independent contractors. The principal's expectations, the skill levels and training of teachers, and the culture of the school are all contributors to the success of instruction in the building.

The importance of a principal's consistent presence in classrooms cannot be stressed enough. A principal should dedicate a minimum of six hours per week for classroom visits, first placing them as a priority on his or her calendar, and then conducting these visits consistently.

On classroom visit days, it may be beneficial for a principal to be absent from the office until the visits are complete. This is recommended because it is often true that once a principal steps in to the office, myriad distractions may keep him or her from the important task of observing instruction. Arrangements should be made with the office staff in advance, advising them that the principal will be in classrooms beginning first thing in the morning.

It is a good practice for a principal to keep a chart showing classrooms that have been visited, in order to visually track and ensure that the principal makes it to all classrooms consistently on a regular basis. Charting helps pinpoint classrooms that have yet to receive visits or have received less attention than others.

> *I am constantly in classrooms. I have different types of walk-throughs. Some are drop-in: I might go in to classrooms for ten minutes. I leave feedback for them [the teachers]. I do what I call administrative walk-throughs with the reading coach. These last ten to fifteen minutes. The reading coach and I debrief after the visit, and then the coach will go back and talk with [the teachers] and I might send an e-mail saying what I like and what I want them to improve.*
>
> —Jason Cameron, National Blue Ribbon Principal, Delaware

When a principal increases instructional visits to classrooms there is often push-back or resistance from teachers who feel uncomfortable having visitors in the classroom, and are particularly unsettled with the notion of an administrator looking over their shoulders. Principals should move gently into such an initiative, but continue to push forward despite such feedback. Over time, the practice of visiting classrooms will become accepted by both teachers and staff.

Faculty members will ultimately come to believe that the principal belongs in their classrooms, and that visits are beneficial to all parties alike: students, teachers, and the principal. Changing perspectives about the presence of the principal in classrooms may take time, patience, dialogue, and an unrelenting desire on the part of the principal to witness what is happening in classrooms in the interest of helping all practitioners improve.

When a principal knows what is and is not happening in classrooms throughout the school, he or she can formulate targeted training designed to help teachers improve their teaching techniques and pedagogies for the betterment of the students.

> *Protect the flow of the learning system with incremental change and improvement efforts. . . . An effective leader must learn from every initiative and then discern how to implement them to the best advantage of the campus. The goal is . . . improvement for student learning.*
>
> —Marty French, National Blue Ribbon School Principal, South Carolina

HOW DOES A PRINCIPAL ENSURE THAT NEEDED CHANGES ARE ACCOMPLISHED?

Effective principals guide staff to build a culture of continuous improvement with student achievement as its focus. But how can a principal know what needs to be changed? The first clue to answering the question "What needs improving?" exists within the walls of classrooms throughout the school.

A principal's critical work begins in classrooms. Outstanding principals examine instruction, observe teaching strategies, and try to gain an understanding of classroom culture throughout the building, with the intent of learning how each teacher in the school is performing.

There are many questions a principal may consider when examining classroom instruction. The questions range from "What is the quality of instruction?" to intervention strategies and myriad other issues related to instructional effectiveness. A list of recommended questions is provided in the appendix.

> *I communicate with teachers constantly and we disaggregate the data together. We looked at the results and instantly recognized and celebrated the results. . . . Having that ability as a leader [is] to recognize that we are a team and we're going to come up with innovative new ideas to make this happen. . . . That the principal is not locked up in her office but is out collaborating with the teachers is important.*
>
> —Lucille Keaton, National Distinguished Principal, Nevada

In addition to determining what is working or not working in classrooms, top principals also need to meet with school leaders to examine data and identify trends. This is helpful in determining how groups of students are doing in specific classes or subjects, or in certain grades, or with certain teachers, and whether the students perform differently under a different set of circumstances.

Analyzing academic strengths and weaknesses among and between subgroups, classes, or groupings of students helps the principal understand the needs of students, teachers, and the school as a whole. A list of recommended questions to consider when examining student performance data is provided in the appendix. Chapter 4 more fully discusses the process of examining student data.

> *I took the time to listen and respond to [staff] concerns when I first arrived at the school three years ago. This has opened many lines of communication and trust within our school. I surveyed every employee and shared the results with the staff the first week on the job. The survey focused on what they believed I needed to do as principal and what they believed needed to be addressed for us to move forward. I then built my goals around what they thought was important my first year. Next, I addressed each one of their concerns and checked them off as we accomplished them.*
> —Dr. Michael P. Lucas, National Blue Ribbon School Principal,
> Pennsylvania

An important step to determine what needs to be changed in a school is to have discussions with staff members. The principal should schedule one-on-one meetings with each member of the faculty or schedule time with small groups of faculty. During the meetings, he or she should take notes of the conversations and also compile findings based on outcomes of the meetings. The notes should focus on subjects mentioned most frequently during the meetings, compiling common themes and areas of potential improvements. A list of recommended questions with which to guide discussion during meetings with faculty and staff is provided in the appendix.

People embrace change at different rates and with different levels of interest. The principal should focus energy on encouraging teachers who can rapidly adopt and implement new or different instructional activities or methodologies. Faculty members who are already successful in the classroom will often be the first to welcome new methods and new ways of teaching. Their support of changes that the principal is trying to implement will essentially transform them into "peer leaders" capable of inspiring their teaching colleagues.

> *Two years ago, I began to consciously build teacher capacity and leadership in my building. I encouraged teachers to explore areas in which they showed curiosity. I encouraged them to share their learning with the entire staff. And then I praised them, loudly, for being a leader in our building. . . . To my delight, I continue to have teachers step up and take leadership roles. . . . It is amazing to see this leadership. I am proud of all of my teacher leaders.*
> —Jackie Meyer, National Distinguished Principal, Idaho

> *A campus cannot afford to stop and re-create the organization every time a new initiative comes into play. It should be guided on a continuous basis to improve. It's kind of like passing a baton on a relay team — you never stop, you just get a fresh leg to keep you moving forward.*
> —Marty French, National Blue Ribbon School Principal, South
> Carolina

MAKING CHANGE POSSIBLE

> *There are three levels of control: no control, remote control, and direct control. Remote control is the primary type of control an administrator exerts. Direct control takes place in the classroom. If you are not teaching, you are exercising remote control. What can I do to increase the likelihood that my message will get out? I am ultimately responsible for what happens in classrooms . . . and yet I have very little direct power to effect the most important changes. How do you ensure that what you want to have happen there [in the classroom] actually happens? You can increase the likelihood via relationships with the teacher and what happens in the classroom. We should expect to see changed behavior. Every year, every adult must get a little better at the work they do.*
> —Dr. Dennis Fox, retired instructional coach, consultant, and special-
> ist, Los Angeles County Division of School Improvement,
> California

Effective principals do their most important work using relationships to guide others, what Fox calls "remote control." Instructional change isn't created in a vacuum. Leaders work with and through others in order to accomplish the goal of instructional improvement.

> *I lead from behind because when I led from the front, I often turned around and found I was alone. Now I plant seeds, we start discussions, and the teachers often think of exactly what I was going to suggest. I have seen many*

expensive initiatives crash and burn when they were not embraced by the staff.
The only way to get people behind something is to get them in front of it.
—Carol Krichbaum, National Blue Ribbon School Principal, Virginia

A principal can exert influence by providing teacher training and re-sources, making expectations known, and building strong, trusting rela-tionships with staff and faculty based on mutual respect. When teachers trust the principal, then his or her guidance, suggestions, and mentoring are more likely to be taken to heart, thus positively impacting instruction.

Guiding instruction is like steering the wheel of a giant ship. You need to be able to start turning the wheel.
—Jonathan A. Ross, National Distinguished Principal, Pennsylvania

Effective school leaders make it their work to establish an expectation of continuous, collaborative instructional improvement throughout the school. Teachers must be persuaded to abandon the concept that they are independent contractors, and instead embrace working together for the benefit of the students. This is done by expecting and making it a practice that instruction, assessment, and data are discussed openly among and between the staff and the principal.

Generally, schools are very comfortable celebrating things like successes, but there is still this weird uncomfortable thing about admitting that they have a challenge. I really think in the heart of teachers they would still be more comfortable closing the door and just working with their kids, and we are trying to open those doors. It really is a cultural shift to encourage people that two heads are better than one.
—Anonymous study participant

Teachers and administrators should view student performance data honestly, transparently, and often. Data review and instructional plan-ning should take place several times a month between teachers, with the principal participating whenever possible. Each grade level teaching team should study, plan, and strategize together using student perfor-mance results to guide next steps, in an effort to create ongoing improve-ments in student success. Assessment and accountability are discussed further in chapter 4.

MOVING FROM IDENTIFIED NEED TO IMPLEMENTED PRACTICE

Change moves more rapidly from innovator to innovator, than from top down.
—Dr. Joe Condon, former superintendent, Lawndale School District,
California

Once a principal and staff have determined what instructional changes are necessary, conclusions should be thoughtfully presented to all staff members. The steps for such presentations should include introducing the instructional changes, teaching them to staff and faculty, modeling the changes, encouraging peer visits, and modeling the changes again.

Introduce

Introduce the concept of the instructional change to the teachers and staff, being careful to ensure that recommendations are presented as positive changes for students and faculty alike. Help the group see the need for the change, rather than simply requiring compliance. Present ideas for improvement in small pieces so that teachers and staff do not become overwhelmed with the changes expected of them.

Teach

In order for school staff to embrace change, they need to understand the process of improvement. Once principals devise changes that will be made, they often make the mistake of taking it as a given that everyone will instinctively know the steps required to implement the changes.

Good principals don't take this for granted. Instead, they take the process apart and break it into smaller components, teaching each part of the process to the staff in ways they will be able to learn and remember.

To the greatest extent possible, principals should actively involve staff members in the learning process. Have staff discuss concepts and ideas with one another. Allow them time to play with and discuss new concepts.

Principals also should be candid with teachers, explaining the challenges that they may face as they implement a new teaching technique or strategy. If change is to flourish, the faculty must feel comfortable with what the principal is asking them to do differently.

Model

It has been said that a picture is worth a thousand words. Having a new concept modeled for any learner is invaluable. When a principal models a new concept in action, the modeling adds impact because teachers see that their leader both understands and can teach and demonstrate the strategy.

Encourage Peer Visits

Encourage teachers to visit one another's classrooms. Ask peers to partner together and take turns modeling lessons. Support this effort by providing teachers with release time, during which their classes may be covered by another staff member. This allows teachers to visit one another during the regular school day.

A principal also may ask teachers to participate in classroom observations, personally showing examples of the desired changes in classrooms where the innovation is already well implemented. During the walkthrough, the principal and teachers may discuss the effect on student instruction in such a way as to improve the teachers' understanding of the new practice. Teachers who have seen a new strategy modeled well in a classroom setting may be more likely to effectively use the strategy themselves.

Model Again!

For instructional change to become well established, teachers may need to see the change in place a number of times in different scenarios and venues. A principal should continue to model and reinforce new strategies that she or he anticipates seeing in classrooms.

Principals should conduct return visits to classrooms to take stock of progress toward newly implemented instructional changes. When teachers know they are being observed, they may exhibit the change in the exact way they have been instructed, or they may show off the change only because they know the principal is looking. Either way, this is a step in the right direction. Faking implementation of a new technique or strategy provides evidence that a teacher understands and is able to implement the requested change, but chooses not to use it consistently.

The principal will need to continue to work with and monitor teachers who are not consistent in implementing recommended changes. If a teacher is not implementing any part of a requested change, the principal will need to determine if the teacher is simply opposing the change, does not understand it, or lacks the ability to make the change or carry out a new teaching strategy. If the issue proves to be defiance on the part of the teacher, a principal may need to counsel with the teacher, and possibly direct him or her to improve. But if the teacher simply does not understand the change, further training is in order.

Finally, if a teacher lacks the ability to make the required change, there is a larger problem. In this case, it is likely that the principal already is working with the teacher to either improve the teacher's performance or encourage the teacher to exit the profession, and should add this issue to the existing list of struggles that the teacher is striving to overcome.

> *We want to make sure our goals are realistic and not overwhelming to the teacher. We talk about what goals we're going to set next and whether or not they are attainable. . . . If [a teacher] comes in and says I'm putting too much pressure on them, I say they might be right, and I might slack off a little on one thing, but then I'll see if we can do something else.*
> —Lucille Keaton, National Distinguished Principal, Nevada

> *I see myself as a caring diagnostician. I am always observing and determining what is not working for individual students and/or staff members. . . . An effective principal maintains an ongoing delicate balance between supporting individuals, helping individuals to realize where they need to grow, and pushing a small minority to realize that their personalities and skills are a better match for a profession other than teaching.*
> —Jan-Marie S. Fernandez, National Distinguished Principal, Virginia

SUMMARY

A school may look stable and unchanging to the casual eye, but in reality it always is evolving. Schools do not remain in static states. Either they improve or they decline. Effective principals ensure that their schools continuously improve.

Before making any changes, effective leaders conduct investigations of classroom practices, collect data, and talk with staff and other interested groups (such as parents) about their attitudes and opinions on the condition of the school's existing instructional delivery system.

Principals seek agreement with teachers about needed changes in instructional practices. Once there is consensus about what needs to be done, the principal formulates a plan to introduce, teach, model, and observe the changes, and then leads the implementation of changes. Top principals ensure that instructional changes move schools in positive directions for the benefit of all students.

Implications for Action

- When determining the course of instructional improvement for a school, a principal and leadership team should spend time in classrooms, examine data, and talk with others about what to change in order to best meet the needs of all students.
- A principal does not directly affect what happens in classrooms. Rather, he or she works by "remote control." In order to have the greatest chance of making a positive impact and steering instruction in the desired direction, a principal must ensure that relationships with staff are solid, positive, and trusting.
- When implementing instructional changes, a principal needs to understand the steps teachers will take to implement the change. In addition, the principal must introduce the concept or strategy in a thoughtful manner, teach it to staff effectively, model it, discuss it at length, and model it again. This incremental process gives teachers the opportunity to observe others who are successfully implementing the change and to implement it themselves.
- The best principals are those who are positive and give support to teachers who are attempting to comply with requested changes, even teachers who implement changes only partially or inconsistently. If a teacher is complying with the principal's requests, it is a step in the right direction—even when a teacher does not yet have new strategies mastered. A principal should counsel with those teachers who cannot or do not implement desired changes.

A STORY FROM THE FIELD

Told by Rhonda Parmer, National Distinguished Principal, Texas

> We had a little girl in the fourth grade named Susan.* She attended our school since pre-kindergarten and struggled all the way through. She always attended tutoring during the day but was not allowed to stay after school for tutoring. We thought it was a cultural thing, or a pride issue with the family.

Every year one of us in the office would "adopt" Susan to go over her homework and just spend ten to twenty minutes talking with her and encouraging her to do her best. She always skimmed by just enough each year to get the passing grades to go on to the next grade level. We winced each year when she was promoted, because we knew of the impending struggles she would surely face.

Susan was small for her age. She is an Asian girl who lived with her dad and two high-school-aged brothers. Her father is a fisherman.

Susan needed glasses. She received a pair every year through the Lions Club, but these were usually lost or broken by the middle of the year. Conferences with dad yielded little results; glasses went unrepaired and homework was never checked at home. In third grade, Susan passed the reading test by one question after staying at school until 6:30 p.m.

In August of 2009, at the urging of her current teacher . . . our intervention team met with her dad with the hope of securing his permission for special education testing. I am sorry to say that it took our team so long to figure out all of these facts. The family was very private and had little time to meet with us. They also had limited English, and Susan was very shy. During the meeting we found out that Susan's mother had left the family when Susan was only two years old. Almost her whole life she had been supervised by her older brothers.

We set up counseling sessions for Susan through . . . our district contacts, and we used the [case]worker to conduct home visits to help her dad learn some parenting skills and find resources. We additionally enrolled Susan in our after-school enrichment program for three hours a day, at no cost to her family. Susan began to make friends, interact in socially appropriate ways like her peers, and even performed with a group of other girls at her end-of-year farewell party.

Amazingly, she ended up earning all As in the last nine weeks of fourth grade, made a 100 percent score on her math [test], and was commended on the reading [test]. Best of all, she grew to know success and the feelings that go along with it. Success breeds success, and her confidence grew in all areas.

She hugged me on the last day of school and said, "I love you. I will miss you. You have been like my mom." I just started heaving and sniffing with huge tears rolling off my face. I did not want to let go of her. I told her how proud I was of her and told her to be sure and invite me to her graduation when she gives the valedictorian speech. She e-mailed me once since she left, to just give me an update of her progress and love for school.

But that did not come from me. She e-mails her teacher . . . about every month to catch up. I really feel that the attention given to her by [her teacher] was what prompted the turnaround in Susan's life. If [her teacher] had not insisted that we do more for her, Susan would have skimmed under the radar for one more year, and who knows how many after that. A great teacher makes all the difference in our students' lives.

*The student's name has been changed and the teacher's name omitted for privacy.

THREE

Building a Culture of Continuous Improvement

It is the role of the school principal to improve the culture of the school, moving toward an ever-increasing focus on student achievement.

The "culture of the school" refers to "the way people do things around here" — specifically, the way people in the organization view and respond to the institution. Adults impact the culture tremendously by conveying to others, both overtly and subtly, the ways they perceive their roles as educators, their perspective on the importance of their work, and the urgency with which they approach their teaching responsibilities.

The belief systems of adults in the education system can have a significant effect on student achievement. If, for example, the adults in the building have a negative view of the school as a whole, this perspective is likely to permeate the manner in which teachers approach their work, which in turn negatively impacts student learning.

If the adults involved with the school view the role of teacher highly, and have a positive opinion about the importance of teaching and learning, these beliefs are likely to have a positive effect for student outcomes.

If educators approach their work with the notion that they have plenty of time in which to accomplish their instructional goals and there is "no rush," there will be little instructional urgency and students will be exposed to concepts on a slower timeline, therefore learning at a slower pace.

The principal is charged with the tasks of determining the status of the culture of the school, and helping to alter the beliefs of the adults involved toward the goal of a new or renewed sense of empowerment. By leading educators toward a belief in the ability of teachers to impact students in positive and significant ways, the principal reminds staff that little is more important to learning than the daily efforts of educators to teach. The principal must help educators understand the urgent need to use every instructional minute for its best and highest possible use, in order to prepare students rapidly and efficiently for exceptional academic experiences.

In addition to promoting positive perceptions of the mission of the school among teachers and staff, the principal also assumes the role of "gatekeeper," allowing things to occur at the school that will positively affect student instruction, and eliminating things that are a hindrance to student achievement.

> *The only reason to think that the students at your school will do any better this year than they did last year, is because the adults who work at your school will figure out what they need to do differently. Every year the adults are expected to get a little bit more effective at their work. If the adults do this year what they did last year, there is no reason to think the students will do any better.*
> —Dr. Dennis Fox, instructional coach, consultant, and specialist, Los Angeles County Division of School Improvement, California

Schools are magnets for time-consuming events such as fundraisers, assemblies designed to increase school spirit, and holiday celebrations— each of which can become a distraction from the focus on student achievement. A principal's role is to maintain the focus on instruction and limit events that take time away from teaching and learning. Protecting instructional time is continuous work, but is of critical importance to schools that hope to make a positive difference in student achievement.

Extracurricular activities have a way of insidiously eating away at critical classroom learning time, a trend requiring principals to constantly protect school-wide core learning time. It is not uncommon for well-meaning adults at the school to plan things that are either more interesting or more fun than solid teaching and learning.

Event organizers may not understand that planning non-instructional events in the middle of the school day has significant negative effects on academic advancement. Principals must be vigilant and unwavering in their efforts to curb interruptions that threaten to monopolize instructional time for non-academic purposes during the school day.

Everyone has a great program they want to bring to your school, but you have to say, "No." I want to be protective of the teachers' teaching time.
  —Sister Marie Blanchette, National Blue Ribbon School Principal,
                  Tennessee

Many programs and events are introduced in school settings with the intent of making the school experience fun for students. One must always weigh, however, whether the experience will enhance opportunities for effective teaching and learning. Before introducing non-academic programs and events, ask if there are any educational benefits to the program. If so, do the supposed advantages outweigh the negative effects of spending time on something other than focused instruction with the classroom teacher?

Rigorous examination of non-academic programming and events is especially important when programs are suggested by outside agencies or well-meaning parent associations. For example, events of this type can range from school carnivals and fundraising assemblies to nonessential school photos and campus-wide recycling programs. The answer that the principal must provide in response to such proposals is "Thank you, but no." When a principal allocates instructional time for non-instructional purposes, the entire school's function and routine is interrupted. Teachers are kept from teaching, and students are prevented from learning.

We have learned the power of the word "No." Any assemblies or field trips must be directly related to the [academic] standards. We continually ask ourselves, "Is this the best use of instructional time?"
  —Dr. Angel J. Barrett, National Distinguished Principal, California

It is all about kids. If it is not impacting kids' learning in a positive way, then we need to be doing something else.
  —W. Fred Crawford, National Blue Ribbon School Principal,
                 South Carolina

It may not easy for a principal to steer faculty and parent groups away from long-standing non-instructional traditions and practices in a school, but it must be done. If the principal cannot help staff cease spending time on things that do not promote instruction, there will be a lack of focus on experiences that make a measurable difference for students academically.

For example, perhaps a school has a long tradition of holding the annual seventh versus eighth grade baseball game during school time. In such a situation, the principal must persuade staff members and parents that however beloved the tradition, it does not promote achievement by the student body as a whole. This may be true for the all-school barbeque, the Halloween parade, and other similar "spirit-building" events.

Remember that focused classroom learning time is critical to student success. Absent a school-wide effort to curb non-instructional interruptions during the academic day, a teacher who hopes to create an instructionally oriented program will suffer constant distractions from other adults who are unable to understand the importance of dedicated instructional time. The principal must, at least initially until the faculty and parent groups understand this key concept, act as "instructional police," vigorously insisting that all staff focus on teaching and learning.

The principal may need to help remove the many enticing distractions teachers create for themselves or for other teachers during the school day. School staff members who truly are focused on teaching will be grateful for the support of the principal in ensuring that teaching time is respected.

Sometimes it is as important to stop unproductive behavior as it is to initiate positive change. One of a principal's first tasks may be to help staff determine what they must do, as well as agree on what they need to stop doing, in order to allow proper time and focus on instruction. This might be called "peeling the onion"—removing layer after layer of "things we've always done" until the school has created a focused instructional program with teaching and learning at its core.

PLANNING EFFECTIVE MEETINGS

Staff meetings should focus on instruction. They are times for the faculty, staff, and principal to together explore topics such as instructional best practices, research results, or new pedagogical approaches to reach different sets of students. Principals need to prevent non-instructional topics from creeping into staff meeting times. Meetings should not be built around a long list of unrelated non-instructional items, but instead should maintain focus on improving teaching and learning.

If a non-instructional agenda item can be reduced to a written memo, then it should be dealt with in that manner. If such an item cannot be written in a memo, it should be relegated to the end of a staff meeting or handled in a way that does not interrupt the instructional focus of the meeting.

One of the best faculty meetings I had we did at the beginning of the school year. I asked the teachers what a . . . graduate should look like. We took all of the responses and typed them. If this is our desired outcome, what do we need to do to get there? From that, the teachers chose their goals for the year.
    —Sister Marie Blanchette, National Blue Ribbon School Principal,
Tennessee

I am big on taking things that teachers have already done and having them present to their colleagues. It is one thing to highlight [accomplishments], to write them notes, and so on. But to put them in front of their colleagues and have them teach them—put my weight behind that—that inspires people to want to do more.
    —Jonathan Ross, National Distinguished Principal, Pennsylvania

If all available staff meeting time is devoted to instructional topics, when should school leaders plan non-instructional events such as the school carnival, soccer tournament, or school dance? A principal can delegate the planning of events to groups or individuals who have time to carry out such work outside of the context of staff meetings. Coordinating and planning school events is important, but it should not be done during staff meetings or professional development times. Principals should reserve staff meetings and training times for the sole purpose of focusing on instruction.

CREATING TIME FOR TEACHER COLLABORATION

As building manager, it is up to me to broker colleague visits, arrange for collaborative planning, and creatively schedule classes to get teachers together and talking about their craft.
    —Dr. Christopher Kennedy, National Distinguished Principal,
Rhode Island

Principals play a key role in building a culture of teacher cooperation and teamwork. When teachers collaborate, they discuss ways to best meet the needs of the students they share. They work with one another to discuss the needs of groups of students who have things in common such as grade or ability levels. Together they create strategies that help each teacher to be as effective as possible in improving instruction.

Collaboration may include the study of assessment data to determine next steps. It may mean planning future lessons together, or speaking with each other about an individual student whom the teachers share in an attempt to best meet a child's needs.

Teacher collaboration is widely accepted as a way to provide support for teachers through teamwork, cooperative planning, and the examination of student data in cooperation with other professionals. Teamwork among educators builds instructional quality and effectiveness by providing several professional points of view and encouraging teacher dialogue and discussion.

Such collaboration could, for example, compare results of one periodic assessment in mathematics to the results of an assessment given six weeks previously, and determine areas of growth as well as areas in which students have not grown as much as the team had hoped.

A team may collaborate to seek explanations as to why some teaching strategies worked and others did not.

Teachers may collaborate around the planning of a unit of study based on a common concept, discussing strategies, lesson delivery, assessments, and creative ideas to make that unit of study more interesting for students.

In order to create and support the efforts of teachers to cooperate and work together, the principal assumes the role of leader and facilitator. The principal works with the team of teachers to identify and prioritize what they hope to accomplish together, and ensures that the teachers understand their shared task. If a group of teachers has agreed to outline the next six weeks of lesson plans for instruction in language arts, for example, a principal may work to ensure that everyone on the team agrees on a common approach and has a plan that the team feels will help guide instruction in the future.

A principal does not need to constantly accompany a collaborative group until their work is completed, but should ensure that each member of the group understands the shared task. The principal also should check the group's progress as members work together. There should be an agreed-on outcome that the group will provide or report to the principal upon completion of the collaboration.

In order to build time for teachers to collaborate and work together, a principal must make every effort to release teachers to take part in collegial discussions with one another during work hours. Such discussions should focus on student progress, the achievement of results, and instruction. Teacher discussions and teamwork may take place before or after class hours, but teacher collaboration often is more meaningful and productive when it takes place during the work day, at times when teachers are less likely to be preoccupied with the coming school day or weary at its end.

> *I arrange time for teachers to interact professionally. By scheduling "common planning time" at least three times each week, professional dialogue is encouraged, which centers on student achievement. Similarly, I arrange for teachers of the same subjects and grade levels to have common preparation periods so they can ensure coherence among their classes and discuss instructional strategies and assess data analysis that help students succeed.*
> —Michael E. Friel, National Distinguished Principal, Lebanon

SCHEDULING TO MAXIMIZE STUDENT ACHIEVEMENT

> *When I got here, everyone was doing their own thing and moving in different directions. We created protected academic time. We have a ninety-minute reading time, plus a forty-five-minute whole-school intervention time when kids are shared. In addition to teaching core programs with fidelity, during the workshop time we provide small group instruction using all adults. . . . We protect academic time.*
> —Bruce E. Reynolds, National Distinguished Principal, Oregon

Effective principals assert a level of control over the school-wide schedule to allow for agreed-upon school-wide instructional efforts. This includes the creation of instructional blocks, which should be designed in collaboration with the faculty.

In an elementary school, for example, when there are common times for core subjects, teachers can share students for instructional purposes. This provides opportunities to assist students according to their academic levels or specific instructional needs. These times may include leveled reading or math instruction, or school-wide intervention time. During these learning blocks, teachers focus on students' specific learning tasks and take student groups depending on the academic needs of the students.

Elementary schools, particularly those in which classes have been self-contained, provide many opportunities for scheduling shifts that enhance learning opportunities. To best manage elementary school schedules, effective principals spend time with staff to determine which instructional blocks are needed and when they should take place.

The timing of key instructional blocks is important. Core academic times should occur first thing in the morning or after a recess break, since these are the optimal times of day when students are rested and ready to learn.

> *You didn't schedule people's days in the past. When I started, [teachers] owned their classrooms. There was no connection between one class of second grade or another. [Now] we believe in providing opportunities for students who need enrichment or remediation through scheduling. You need to have time for teachers and kids to have intervention or enrichment time. If you don't do that, you'll never get your schedule together. Bottom line: you have to sell it to [teachers] because it's best for kids.*
>
> —Sanford E. Nelson, National Distinguished Principal, Minnesota

When elementary school teachers are accustomed to controlling their own instructional blocks, school-wide scheduling of instructional blocks may be difficult. A principal may need to help staff understand that changes to a school's schedule are instructionally beneficial, and that the modifications that are being made to the schedule will have positive effects for teaching and learning.

In secondary schools, principals should examine school-wide schedules to ensure that instructional blocks involving core subjects are provided to students during optimal times of the day. For example, if a teacher teaches more than one subject, such as history and physical education, it may be possible to begin that teacher's day with history and end it with physical education. Secondary teachers share students throughout the day, which means that it is not always possible to place core subjects in student schedules when the students are most fresh. However, the school schedule should be examined for this possibility.

When students are to be shared between teachers, whether in elementary or secondary schools, the principal must work to create common agreements about the length of time students spend moving from class to class, as well as agreements between teachers about their expectations for student conduct during these transitions. Agreements of this type create a set of school-wide expectations, which reduce conflict among teachers and enhance student learning by narrowing the amount of time spent in transition between classes.

UNDERSTANDING INSTRUCTIONAL URGENCY

Protecting instructional time is an important aspect of my job. I ensure that teachers have every possible moment to be in the classroom, uninterrupted with their students.
　　　　—Jacquelyn Meyer, National Distinguished Principal, Idaho

Efforts at school improvements must focus on the allocation of instructional time. A principal must ensure that teachers understand the importance of spending academic blocks wisely.

"Instructional urgency" is the notion that there is no time to waste, that every minute of every educational day is critical, and that teaching time is a valuable and perishable resource.

Educators who teach effectively and efficiently, minimize interruptions, and ensure quick transitions from one activity to another are ones who understand instructional urgency. Such teachers insist on consistently making the best and smartest use of their time. They make supplies like books, pencils, and paper readily available to students in order to minimize time spent distributing materials, for example. Routine movements of students, such as a daily transfer from reading to math class, or from one area of the classroom to desks, are practiced and perhaps even timed until they can be done as quickly as possible. In the classrooms of teachers who understand instructional urgency, every minute counts.

Principals who wish to promote an understanding of instructional urgency create systems, practices, and protocols to ensure students get right to work in their classrooms once they arrive at school. Practices such as how students line up in the morning, how attendance is collected and recorded, and the way in which transition times are orchestrated send strong messages from the principal to the students and staff that time is considered a valuable instructional resource not to be wasted.

Principals wishing to minimize classroom interruptions should examine telephone policies. When and how often do office staff, parents, other teachers, or even the principal call teachers during instructional blocks? Is the telephone only used for important messages from parents to students, or is it used whenever a request is made? Can calls to classrooms be delayed until non-instructional times of day? Can calls from parents or inquiries for a teacher be handled by the principal or office staff during the instructional block? Curtailing phone calls to classrooms during the instructional day will enhance teachers' ability to focus on their students by minimizing interruptions.

Telephone policies vary from school to school. Some principals simply prohibit the main office from calling classrooms during instructional time. Others designate the last five minutes of the period before lunch, or the last five minutes before the end of the school day, as permissible call times. Still others send important messages to teachers using e-mail, and ask faculty to check e-mail only during breaks or at the end of a class.

> *I went to great labors to make certain that outside lines did not ring directly into classrooms. Calls that need to go into classrooms go through the office. If teachers need to call each other in their classrooms, we make sure the other person does not have children in their room at the time.*
> —Robert Slane, National Blue Ribbon School Principal, Wisconsin

> *We've set up a culture of no interruptions. . . . There are no phone calls, no ringing of telephones into classrooms. Staff members in the front office are told that the message will be sent by a note taken to the child, instead of calling. The office staff walks notes out . . . and we get it straight to the classroom. One you've made that a school policy and the community knows you're following through with that, and you're dependable about getting the notes to the kids, they relax and abide by the rules of the school.*
> —Brian M. Hull, National Distinguished Principal, Virginia

Another way to curb classroom disruptions is to avoid the use of the public address system for non-emergency announcements. Public all-call announcements are an interruption, and rarely are they relevant enough to be worth interrupting all teachers throughout the school. A principal should find alternative ways to communicate with teachers and students and should not use the public address system as a daily form of communication.

> *If I had wire cutters and knew I wouldn't electrocute myself, I would snip the wires of the public announcement systems. They are simply too tempting. Adults hoping to find someone on campus can barely resist the urge to jump on the PA system and interrupt seven hundred students in one fell swoop. We have to get our announcement systems under control, and in my mind that means either break them or have one person authorized to use them. That person should be someone who can discern a true emergency situation. Other than that, what could possibly be important enough to interrupt instruction for your entire student population?*
> —Linda K. Wagner (author of this book)

Not all participants in this study agreed with the notion of curtailing all public announcements. Many principals use morning announcements, but keep the broadcast short and do not use the public address system again during the school day.

Whatever option a principal chooses, he or she should limit use of the public address system and carefully consider whether an announcement is important enough to warrant the instructional interruption.

> *Morning announcements last no longer than three minutes and take place as soon as the tardy bell rings. Any other announcements that must take place throughout the day are left until the last five minutes of the day. . . . We block our instructional time so that students who receive services through an Individualized Education Plan are not missing critical learning time in their general education classroom. This year we cut back our lunch time, giving teachers an additional five minutes of instructional time. My staff is especially talented at using every spare minute to practice instructional skills. As students wash hands and line up for lunch, teachers are using math fact and vocabulary cards. . . . It is my responsibility to protect their time with students to ensure that as much learning as possible is taking place each day.*
> —Jacquelyn Meyer, National Distinguished Principal, Idaho

EXTENDING THE SCHOOL DAY OR YEAR

> *I am fortunate to have a staff so willing to put in the additional time to help students. Many of them also give up their prep period to assist students. I lead by example in making sure teachers know that the time they are here is vital for helping students. I am at school every morning at 5:30 and teachers begin coming in around 6 to 6:30 to prepare for the day. Students are actually in our building sitting around the lunchroom tables around 6:30 and are studying until the first bell rings at 8:05. . . . Our students see the importance of an education and are going to do their part in their preparation for college.*
> —Wayne C. Roellich, National Blue Ribbon School Principal,
> Washington

Academic achievement can be enhanced by adding time to the school day, thereby increasing learning time for students. The principal and his or her team should attempt to find ways to add to the school day with before-school, after-school, or evening instruction, by shortening lunch, or by lengthening the school day when possible.

A principal may not have much control over the length of the school day because of collective bargaining contracts with teachers or unions;

however, initiating the conversation and discovering the limits presently imposed on the length of the school day is worthy of study. Such an effort may lead to creative additional instructional opportunities for students.

A principal may determine if opportunities exist for students to supplement their educational experiences through the addition of school days to the calendar year. Also worth exploring are creative ideas to add instructional opportunities through summer school, inter-session classes, and classes that are held during holiday breaks. Staff and parent groups may be persuaded of the benefits of such additional opportunities for students once the principal explains that they lead to increased academic results.

SUMMARY

The principal plays a key role in maintaining the focus on instruction throughout the school. As the instructional leader, a principal must make an in-depth and ongoing examination of instructional and non-instructional practices throughout all levels of the organization. As a principal carries out this examination, visits to classrooms become integral for leading and achieving lasting and positive academic change.

Effective principals help teachers make the very best use of instructional time. They plan for teacher collaboration and help teachers work together on issues of student achievement. When educators work together to discuss assessments, instructional delivery, and student needs, their work tends to show positive results for the students they serve.

Holding focused, instruction-oriented staff meetings is vital to building the effectiveness and capacity of teachers. Principals must use meeting time wisely and conduct non-instructional discussions outside of staff meeting time.

A principal should focus on attempting to provide the maximum amount of learning time for students, curtailing interruptions whenever possible. A principal ensures that there is uninterrupted academic time during which teachers may work intensively with their students.

The principal should share and encourage the concept of "instructional urgency," helping teachers understand the importance of each teaching moment and each opportunity to improve instruction. Focused academic time with students is of utmost importance when building systems designed to improve student achievement.

In elementary schools, a principal should create school-wide schedules that allow students' academic needs to be met through sharing of students among teachers and should use data to group students in order to best meet instructional needs.

Explore opportunities to extend the school day or year. If possible, principals may find ways to add instructional days, after-school opportunities, summer school, or other additional opportunities for learning that will enhance students' instructional experiences.

Implications for Action

Effective principals do the following:

- Create time in the school's daily schedule for teacher collaboration and planning.
- Help teachers understand that every minute they are with students is an opportunity for teaching and learning.
- Encourage teachers to develop keen attention to time, and shore up classroom practices to minimize non-instructional activities during the school day.
- Create school-wide elementary school schedules that promote the best use of instructional time, allow students to transition to those teachers who are best equipped to meet their unique needs during specific times of the day, and ensure that transitions are efficient and orderly.
- Create policies that reduce classroom interruptions during instructional blocks, including limiting the use of telephone calls and public announcements during class time.
- Recognize that the principal is an essential force behind efforts to reduce distractions to the teaching and learning process.
- Consider opportunities to extend the school day or the school year for supplemental instruction, such as creating before-school, after-school, or evening classes; adding school days to the calendar; or utilizing extended-year learning opportunities like summer school or inter-session classes.
- Ensure that the entire school culture supports student achievement.

- Work with staff members to determine what actions they can take to best support the academic goals of the school.
- Determine what the school needs to start doing, and be emphatic about what the school needs to stop doing, in order to focus on student achievement.
- Work with staff to eliminate nonessential programs that distract from instruction.
- Make staff meetings a time to introduce, teach, and reinforce good instructional practices.

A STORY FROM THE FIELD

Told by Jacquelyn Meyer, National Distinguished Principal, Idaho

We had an adorable young Hispanic boy by the name of Javier.* Javier was very shy for his age, but he loved school and both of his teachers. Javier's parents were immigrants, working for a local landscape nursery. Javier benefited both from breakfast and lunch at school, as well as the clothes, shoes, and a winter coat that we provided for him through a local organization.

Because they were not in the country legally, Javier's family did not have a Social Security number or any medical or dental insurance. Without legal status, Javier's family could not access social services in our community. For Javier this was tragic. Javier had a mouth full of rotting teeth. Many of his baby teeth had already broken off at the roots and many others were very infected. Often Javier had a difficult time eating and was sick, running a fever because of the infections in his mouth.

Soon after the school year started, Javier wormed his way into my heart. When the school nurse had me look into his mouth, I was sick with horror that this young boy was living with this pain and infection. How could a child learn English when his mouth was in constant pain? How unfair is our world when little five-year-old boys are denied dental health and medical coverage and my children are wearing braces so their teeth will be as white and perfectly straight as possible? Certainly it was not Javier's fault that his family was trying to provide a better life for him and his siblings—though illegally—in the United States.

I called my dentist. I begged him to examine Javier to see if he could help in any way. I am sure the dentist could hear the passion in my voice and he quickly agreed to see Javier in his office that afternoon. Our on-site Spanish interpreter called Javier's mom and she agreed to have the dentist examine Javier. With Javier belted into a child's booster seat we left school and stopped at the family apartment to pick up Javier's mother. While the language barrier was a problem (I do not speak Spanish and Javier's mom does not speak English), I quickly understood that Javier's mom was extremely thankful for the help that her son would receive.

The dentist could not have been more helpful and patient. Javier was not sure that he wanted this strange man looking into his mouth! With my assurance, Javier quickly settled down and Dr. Stevens examined Javier. I could tell by the look on the dentist's face that he had never examined a child's mouth that was in this condition before. We quickly found a Spanish interpreter and the dentist shared with Javier's mom that he was overwhelmed and was not the right doctor to deal with all of the issues in Javier's mouth. He offered to call a pediatric oral surgeon, a close colleague of his. With the same passion that was heard in my voice, the dentist convinced the oral surgeon to see Javier the next afternoon.

As you can imagine, the outcome of this story is a heart-warmer. Through a series of appointments and one surgery to remove all of Javier's teeth, Javier was fitted with pediatric dentures that would get him through until his adult teeth grew in. Within two weeks, Javier was back at school with a full set of beautiful, white teeth that allowed him to play, eat, and learn without pain.

Javier's success does not belong to me alone—it often takes an entire village to raise a child.

*The student's name has been changed for privacy.

FOUR

Using Data to Guide Instruction

In God we trust. All others bring data.

— W. Edwards Deming

Data is an aggregation of information by which educators assess student academic growth. Data can be gathered from a variety of sources, including standardized and content-based testing, attendance and disciplinary records, and observation of students, to name a few. Various data measurements taken at any given time may provide a baseline from which, it is anticipated, students will grow and improve.

Why examine student data? Student data provides vitally important information about the progress and depth of student learning, which helps educators develop strategies to advance each child's individual achievement. Data can indicate to teachers the most useful strategies by which instructional goals can be accomplished, given each student's response to prior learning opportunities. Group summary data also helps educators focus on the achievement needs of the group of students as a whole.

When educators examine student data, they may be able to determine which students are learning at an appropriate pace and which are not. The data also may help identify the concepts that students who are not reaching the classroom median are failing to grasp.

Variance from benchmarks may indicate what subgroups of students need additional help, at what grade levels different students tend to do better or worse, and which teachers consistently receive better test results. Data points can be used in the analysis of progress for the school, for teachers, for grade levels, subgroups, genders, and for individual students.

Like attempting to diet without a scale, instructing students without measuring results becomes merely a random act. Data is necessary for teaching to acquire a laser-like focus on student achievement. Relentless examination of student data is a key strategy by which principals are able to measure the success of students, teachers, their schools, and even their own work.

Trends can be ascertained by analyzing data from grade levels and individual classrooms and making comparisons throughout the year, and from year to year. This kind of analysis over time may be highly instructive, but the principal should remember that there often will be data points that are "outliers," or anomalies—such as the odd year in which achievement spikes or drops at a grade level with no apparent root cause. Such unique spikes or drops in achievement should not be a major cause for concern. However, if comparisons and trends of data from year to year seem to indicate areas in which students are not being successful, or if there are continuing low overall scores in a particular class or grade level, the principal must intervene.

> *Data is the key to making effective instructional decisions. . . . The purpose of assessing [data] is to determine what has been learned. It guides teacher planning for small-group instruction, tutoring, and when to move to new learning concepts. Data reflects the position of a child on the learning continuum of a curriculum strand. If we want the child to improve, then we meet the child on his or her level and move them forward. Instruction becomes very specific for the individual. Teachers who don't reflect on assessment data are teaching their curriculum, not the child. Most children will learn from teaching the curriculum, but many will get lost, get bad grades, and try to "study harder." They may never get the one or two lessons of intervention that could fill in the gap of understanding.*
>
> —Marty French, Blue Ribbon School Principal, South Carolina

WHOSE JOB IS IT TO WORK WITH STUDENT DATA?

Data analysis is the means by which one determines the changes that are needed to bring about academic improvement. A principal may believe that students learning English need more time to work on language development, for example, but without data to either confirm or disprove that theory, the principal is merely guessing. The gathering and study of student data is imperative for any school leader who hopes to create positive instructional change throughout the organization.

> *Back up hunches with good data.*
> —Dr. Jane Koberlein, National Distinguished Principal, Missouri

A principal should analyze data in collaboration with teacher grade level or cohort staff teams in order to best determine what instructional changes are needed in order to move student achievement to higher levels. Data review should be a frequent, recurrent study that involves the principal, staff, students, and parents.

If a principal does not participate in data review, it is likely the faculty will assume one of two things: either the principal does not know how to work with data or the principal does not consider this work to be important. No principal wants to send either of these messages to staff or constituents.

A principal who strives to be an instructional leader should create a year-long ongoing plan to gather data, make regular analyses of the results of the data, and hold frequent meetings with staff to make instructional adjustments based on conclusions drawn from the data. Each data meeting may cover a different topic, ensuring that over the course of a school year time is devoted to all subgroups of students, grade levels, cohorts, and gender groups. Another crucial topic for a data meeting is a review of disciplinary and attendance data.

Principals can use achievement data to guide changes to the school-wide instructional program. They also may use student data to motivate others to build a culture of continuous improvement, with student achievement at its core. Principals can point to data to provide encouragement to staff and to show parents and students solid evidence of the need for improved student achievement.

Disciplinary data may be used to examine the effects and outcomes of disciplinary referrals to the school office during times when students are in class, in another example. Also, attendance rates can be discussed with parents, teachers, and students as one way to motivate learners to come to school with greater frequency.

There are myriad examples of how working with student data is important in improving student success. All of them point to the fact, however, that principals must roll up their sleeves and work beside teachers in the analysis of student data in order to build school systems designed around continuous academic improvement.

> *As principal, I work to know and understand the needs of each one of our five-hundred-plus students. I pore over the monthly data looking for those students who are falling behind. I monitor what we are doing to meet their needs. . . . My job is to make sure the appropriate placement assessments have been completed and to ensure that students are placed in the appropriate grade levels and programs to meet their needs. It is also my responsibility to be the advocate for the needs of students.*
>
> —Kay L. Collins, National Distinguished Principal, Colorado

While it is important for the principal to take the lead in working with student data, involving teachers also is critically important. Teachers should participate in the effort to examine, compile, and boil down data to kernels of truth that lead to action. This is done through a process of discernment conducted by the principal and involving active engagement by teachers, staff, students, and parents.

Some principals may wish to closely oversee the creation of reports, charts, and graphs instead of delegating this work to others. This may be a fine line to walk, however, because if a principal takes too much of this function away from faculty, they will lack a strong sense of the school's results.

If teachers do not actively participate in tracking student progress, they will not be in a position to add emphasis to areas in which they may be able to improve instruction. If they are not aware of each child's data compared with peers of the same age group, teachers cannot effectively assess next steps to help remediate a child's academic shortfalls.

Although it is definitely the principal's function to ensure that data is gathered, it is the instructional team's job to ensure that it is correctly and thoroughly assessed. All educators in the team, including the principal, benefit students when they are involved in data review and take action to adjust the academic experience for students according to their findings.

> *It's about relationships and good instruction. It's not about using data to beat teachers over the head.*
>
> —Andrew M. Doell, National Blue Ribbon School Principal, New York
>
> *We have mapped all the content areas of our curriculum, so we constantly review where we are and where we need to be in every area. At our school, we have a data team comprised of teachers who love and respect data as much as I do. We begin by compiling all the data and analyzing it to improve instruc-*

tion. *Once you take the focus off the teacher and pinpoint where the strengths and weaknesses lie, then the data team is able to pinpoint where improvement is needed. Using standardized test scores, we determine relative weaknesses and change direction within the curriculum if needed. . . . We then dig down and review each student's achievement and where he or she falls within the grade. In this way, we are able to teach to each student's strength and add support for areas that are weak. Tweaking the curriculum and re-evaluating the time spent in various areas of the school will help us all make the best use of our time.*

—Dr. Joann Borchetta, National Distinguished Principal, Connecticut

DATA DRIVES IMPROVEMENT RESULTS

The challenge of the data: student achievement should reflect that we're getting better at our profession of teaching. The common goal for student success inspires us to work together to improve our skills. It thrills me to observe teachers getting passionate about student learning.

—Marty French, National Blue Ribbon School Principal, South Carolina

As the principal, leadership team, grade-level groups, and parents work frequently and consistently with student data, they will begin to ascertain trends. Some student groups will improve from the benchmark, and teachers will see evidence of a level of success. Other student groups may not progress. Data may show some subgroups of students lagging in general, while other data may indicate that some students are consistently failing to make progress in specific academic areas.

If data leads principals to discern a lack of progress or a widening of achievement gaps among given student populations, it is important not to blame the students. It is the instructional team that must come to school prepared to meet the needs of their students, not the students who must come to school prepared to meet the needs of their teachers. Consistently gathering and analyzing school-wide student performance data allows a principal to devise effective plans for the school staff to execute, in order to help students reach achievement goals.

Occasionally, a teacher may try to explain educational shortcomings by citing a student's home life or other factors outside the school's control as the reason for delays in achievement. A wise principal will encourage this teacher to change focus and pay attention instead to the parts of the child's experience that are within the educator's control. Ensuring that children are safe at school, making sure they are provided with a high-quality educational experience, and clearly demonstrating to children that there is at least one adult at the school who cares deeply about them are all within the power of every faculty and staff member.

> I spoke up in a data meeting and said, "I just want to point something out from looking at the data. As I look, it is true that we only have over 50 percent of our kids scoring at level 3 or 4, but if you look closely at the kids who scored 2, most of them were really close! What that tells me is there is a large percentage of kids that are really close to making it." I would venture to guess that if we looked at those kids, many of them have tough home situations, are not engaged at school, and have things in their lives that you and I would have trouble dealing with. What can we do with that population to make an impact? Find "gray area" kids and get to know them. Do they play baseball? Go to a game. Try to build relationships with parents. Give them more time and attention.
> —Andrew M. Doell, National Blue Ribbon School Principal, New York

The principal must work with the staff to set measurable goals for student achievement by seeking out and using specific data points and then devising plans targeted at improving student performance. For instance, teachers may see that students who are part of a certain socioeconomic subgroup are performing more poorly in language skills than they are in math. Using observational and numerical data can lead to effective goal-setting to close this gap, based on concrete knowledge of the progress these students are making.

> Teachers complained about the length of the assessment, that it was a waste of instructional time. I said, "I'm going to challenge your thinking. It's not a waste. Without those assessments, you are shooting in the dark in terms of what that child needs instructionally. By spending time with that child you can pinpoint instruction."
> —Andrew M. Doell, National Blue Ribbon School Principal, New York

Once the team identifies what needs to be improved, a school-wide effort should be made to prepare staff to meet the identified needs of the students. Professional development activities should focus on areas of widespread student weakness. Coaching by lead teachers and the principal should be aligned toward the same school-wide goals. In all areas, but particularly with at-risk or lower achieving groups of students, student performance data should become a catalyst for change in instructional practices to best meet student needs.

STUDENT AND PARENT INVOLVEMENT WITH DATA

It is helpful to have students track their own academic progress. Depending on the age of children, they can be involved in monitoring their own data at different levels and amounts of detail. Using simple bar graphs for kindergarteners, working up to deeper examination of specific data points as children move from upper elementary grades through high school, can be very informative as well as motivating for students.

Having the opportunity to review their own data helps students understand areas in which they need to improve, especially when this information is used in conjunction with regular student conferences with the classroom teacher. This process helps students proactively create goals for their own progress and enables them to share their own personal academic improvement targets with their teachers and parents.

When students are clear about the areas in which they need to improve, they often become motivated to work harder in those areas. Principals should encourage student involvement in the assessment of their own performance data and encourage teachers to work with students to set academic goals for their progress.

Parents should be made aware of their child's academic performance data, both on standardized tests and on regular benchmark assessments. These benchmark tests ought to be given at least every six weeks to three months throughout the school year, in order to provide parents and teachers an ongoing and unbiased measure upon which to base discussions about a child's areas of strength and challenge. Once data becomes available, it should be shared with parents, preferably one-on-one in a parent/teacher conference. This forum allows teachers and parents an opportunity to collaborate in their support of the student's improvement.

Parents who understand their child's assessment data can provide targeted help and support at home. Based on the data, they may choose to help the student practice in weaker skill areas, seek tutoring, or add opportunities for learning outside the school day. Parents who are apprised of their child's performance data can become strong partners in the education of the child.

Many parents will not want to delve deeply into a review of school-wide data, but summaries should be made available to the parents. In such summaries, all personal data must be treated as confidential, but parents should be allowed to compare their child's progress with that of other children at the school. Making school-wide data available to parents will give them the opportunity to compare on a micro level (their child versus grade-level peers) and on a macro level (how the school is doing compared with other similar schools).

SUMMARY

Data gathering and examination should be an activity in which principals, staff, parents, and students engage. Principals need to operate in concert with staff to conduct an evaluation and analysis of student data in order to best align instructional efforts with student needs. Examination of data sorted by gender, ethnic groups, attendance rates, discipline, and other measurable non-academic indicators should be conducted when possible.

Once trends are noted, strategies can be developed to achieve immediate instructional goals as well as to strategically plan future academic programs, professional development, and instructional efforts. Students can benefit from tracking their own progress, and parents can become active supporters of their child's academic efforts through frequent opportunities to review and discuss their child's progress in school.

Implications for Action

- The collection and analysis of data creates a kind of measuring stick to help determine whether what is being taught in the school is being learned, and by whom.
- Educators may rely on the interpretation of student data to understand the effects of instruction on student results.
- When compared over the course of a year or from year to year, student data will help principals determine which teachers tend to be effective and in what areas. Such data will help principals encourage those teachers who show solid student performance results and coach those who do not.
- Principals, teachers, students, and parents should be involved in the analysis of student data.
- It is helpful for students to be given the opportunity to track their own data, enabling them to recognize and articulate areas in which they need to improve.

- Parents should be made aware of their child's progress. They should have opportunities to examine their child's test results and compare them with the trends of their child's peer group. This helps parents understand their child's progress and assist their child at home.

A STORY FROM THE FIELD

Told by Bruce Cannard, National Distinguished Principal, Washington

A teacher brought a student to the office. We have Response to Intervention (RTI) across our building. He was in a new reading group. He was slow and unwilling to participate. His name was José.* He wouldn't talk.

I asked him about himself. He said "I don't like my class." I asked him why. He was in a dual language class and in leveled reading. He was uncomfortable in leveled reading because he was away from the kids he was accustomed to being with. I sensed something more was happening.

I asked, "What if next Monday you pick a good friend of yours in your dual language class and then you pick some kids you might know from the new class, and let's talk during lunch. I have a bunch of games. Just invite them and we'll get to know a little bit about them, and let them get to know a little bit about you. I think you're uncomfortable because you just don't know some of the kids."

After this, he just lit up, and started to participate. His teacher said, "I don't know what you did for José, but he sure is excited!"

*The student's name in this story has been changed for privacy.

FIVE

Personnel: Hiring and Retaining Only the Best

We expected that good-to-great leaders would begin by setting a new vision and strategy. We found instead that they first got the right people on the bus, the wrong people off the bus, and the right people in the right seats on the bus—and then they figured out where to drive it. The old adage, "People are your most important asset," turns out to be wrong. People are not your most important asset. The right people are.

—J. Collins, Good to Great (2001), p. 13

SELECTING THE RIGHT PEOPLE

The principal's ability to improve the quality of classroom instruction lies almost completely in the ability to hire well and support teachers in their efforts to be effective in the classroom.

Most principals, however, arrive at school sites that are already fully staffed. Their skills and abilities, both individually and collectively, are firmly established. Therefore, personnel work—the task of creating the most effective team possible—is essential work. It is an effort that takes place little by little, teacher by teacher, as slots open at the school, in cooperation with a staff that already exists and may have a long collective history at the site. So how does the principal influence the makeup of the staff?

When a new principal arrives at a school site, the new leader must assess the effectiveness of the teaching staff. The principal needs to spend significant time observing instruction in order to gauge the skill levels and abilities of the teachers, examining areas of strength and weakness, and compiling information that allows the principal to make recommendations for improvement.

Encouraging all teachers toward best practices and counseling ineffective teachers to improve or leave the profession may be the most important work of the school principal, and can have tremendous impact on the quality of instruction in classrooms throughout the school.

> *Hiring well allows the principal to be a visionary for the school. If I have the right people in the classrooms, I can do my job.*
> —Sister Marie Blanchette, National Blue Ribbon School Principal,
> Tennessee

WHICH TEACHERS SHOULD RECEIVE THE MOST ATTENTION?

A principal should spend the majority of his or her time and effort helping effective teachers to continuously improve. This may appear counterintuitive, as many principals feel drawn to helping poorer performing teachers increase their skills.

When properly encouraged, supported, and trained, however, top performers will not only teach students effectively but also quickly learn new teaching skills. They also may be successful in altering the culture of a school and leading other teachers to join them in expecting high performance in new and existing areas of instructional expertise.

As a principal helps top-level teachers improve, a critical mass of trained experts will develop in the school. This increasingly significant group of educators may be ready, willing, and able to help other educators grow and improve.

Rather than pushing, pulling, prodding, and threatening the naysayers, an effective principal spends time with those teachers who have the talent and attitude to progress in areas in which the principal wants to lead change efforts. Staff members may read these signals from the principal, and follow the lead of the energetic and motivated teachers out of fear that they will be left behind. Changes in school culture will follow, and may even start to take on a life of their own, with initiation from an energetic group of good teachers.

Poorer performing teachers will always need help, support, and coaching in order to improve, but a wise principal starts with energetic, successful teachers. The principal should make it a habit to spend a majority of available time ensuring that effective, positive teachers are as successful as possible.

> *We tend to give power to negative people by concentrating on them, spending time on them. . . . When someone comes to me and wants money out of the budget, they are not going to get it if they are not positive. . . . I've taken away people's leadership when they weren't the best. . . . Sometimes it works to make someone uncomfortable and they will leave.*
>
> —Study participant, name intentionally omitted

> *Hire the best people, put them in the right positions, and get out of the way.*
> —Jonathan A. Ross, National Distinguished Principal, Pennsylvania

HIRING PERSONNEL

> *Hiring personnel: Rule 1: Never hire clones of yourself. Rule 2: Always check references. Rule 3: Take the time to look through the candidate's portfolio. Rule 4: Always schedule an on-site observation of the potential candidate actually teaching. If a new teacher, invite them to substitute for a class or be a guest teacher. Rule 5: Let the teaching partner of the potential candidate be a part of the interview process.*
>
> —Dr. Jane Koberlein, National Distinguished Principal, Missouri

In her guidance, Dr. Koberlein provides key advice. It is human nature to instinctively favor hiring people who mirror our own skills and abilities, or even our own personality style. When a principal hires, however, he or she should look for people with diverse perspectives, abilities, and strengths, seeking those whose skills complement the team. The resulting differences among staff members will enrich discussions and dialogue, and provide unexpected opportunities to learn and grow through the contribution of different points of view and approaches to teaching and learning.

> *Everyone brings something different to the table. Not everyone needs to look like me, sound like me, and think like me. We need people whose skills and talents can extend the work.*
>
> —W. Fred Crawford, National Blue Ribbon School Principal,
> South Carolina

Check references. Not only should principals make phone calls to talk with the listed references of new hires, but they also should call people who know the candidate but who may not appear on the candidate's reference list.

If the teacher has worked at a given school and did not list the principal, there may be a reason for this. Call the former principal to find out what he or she has to say about the candidate. Identify other reliable people with whom the teacher candidate may have worked and call three people who are not listed as references. The results may be very informative, particularly if a candidate has struggled in previous employment.

If the candidate has professional paperwork or a portfolio, take the time to examine the document. Contents of the portfolio will be helpful in gaining a sense of the background and work experience of the candidate. A principal also may learn about the candidate's attention to detail and orderliness by examining the manner in which this professional paperwork is presented.

If the principal chooses to examine the portfolio, this should not be done during the interview. Ask the candidate for permission to keep the portfolio for twenty-four hours. When there is a quiet opportunity, examine its contents. Reading a portfolio during an interview distracts the team from listening carefully to the candidate, and can be a significant disruption to the interview process.

Interview teacher candidates by watching them teach. Include model lessons as part of the interview process. This step is commonly skipped. However, watching a candidate interact with a group of students will help the team learn far more about the teacher's ability to perform than any across-the-desk interview ever could, and is highly recommended.

Invite teacher leaders, and especially those with whom the teacher candidate will be working closely, to have input into the hiring process. While the principal makes the ultimate hiring decision, the input of future colleagues, and especially potential teacher partners, can add a variety of perspectives and address questions and issues the principal may not have considered.

There are a number of systems principals use to include staff members in the process of selecting teachers to work at a school site. What follows is one principal's approach to including teachers in the process:

> I initially had a meeting with anyone who wanted to have input on who we are going to hire. We talked about the characteristics we wanted to see in future teachers. Then I said, "We are going to appoint some grade-level representatives who are going to look at résumés. Then we are going to narrow the group

even further to one per grade level, and then we will interview from that group." That was great because at the first meeting maybe six or seven showed up, and we had a great conversation. We asked, "What are we looking for?" And we listed them and said it was the lens through which we would look for future teachers.

We came up with the criteria and I shared it with the staff. Then we began to look at résumés. And that was an interesting piece, because I said, "I want you to flag résumés that represent these qualities." I saw some résumés that were flagged that did not represent the qualities we had discussed, but they were local people. I said "Is this really someone who reflects these qualities?" Then we had a great conversation about how we're not hiring somebody because they put in their time, we are hiring someone because our students deserve the best.

Teachers were concerned that if we hired the best, they would just leave in a year. So I said, "Well, if we hire them because they are the best, and they leave after a year, we hire the best replacement person. We are not going to stick kids with mediocrity. . . ." It got around that we value great teachers, not service or longevity, or other factors. We don't hire the most popular. That set an important tone.

—Andrew M. Doell, National Blue Ribbon School Principal, New York

RETAINING PERSONNEL

Rule 1: Give your staff the respect, guidance, and support they deserve. Rule 2: Show appreciation. Rule 3: Provide opportunities for professional growth. Rule 4: Be open to listening to suggestions and concerns. Rule 5: Provide a safe, clean, and comfortable working environment.

—Dr. Jane Koberlein, National Distinguished Principal, Missouri

Respect the employees, and top performers in particular. Allow them to do their best work without getting in their way. Interact with them with trust whenever possible, in order to create a staff that is confident in their own abilities and in their relationship with their principal.

Appreciation goes a long way. Teachers enjoy being noticed, thanked for a job well done, supported in their efforts, and rewarded, even in small ways. Principals who leave positive notes, thank people personally, set up small receptions and gatherings to honor special accomplishments or events, and are thoughtful about acknowledging staff members contribute to teachers' feelings of connectedness and a sense of well-being in the school.

Encourage professional growth. Educators not only want to grow continually in their practice, but they also need to keep learning in order to keep up with the changing demands of their profession. Make professional growth opportunities available to teachers to help them keep their skills applicable, current, and effective.

Listen to suggestions and concerns. Gather the opinions of others. Implement the ideas of staff members when possible. Teachers come to believe they have power in the decision-making process at the school when they see their suggestions implemented. This in turn contributes to teachers' feelings of connectedness and worth at the school, where they may begin to contribute more frequently because they feel they are making a difference and impacting campus-wide decision making.

A safe, clean, and comfortable working environment is essential. Teaching and learning is most effective when teachers and students feel safe and comfortable. If the roof leaks or there is evidence of mice in the building, staff members and students will become uneasy. If classrooms are too hot or too cold because heating systems are not functioning properly, the comfort of both students and staff is compromised. The principal should take steps to ensure that maintenance issues are handled quickly in order to maintain a safe, clean, and sanitary school.

Retaining teachers requires a mixture of many things from a principal. Included among them are good leadership, involvement of teachers in decision making, the opportunity for staff to grow professionally, always extending thanks for a job well done, and maintenance of a friendly and clean campus. Savvy principals ensure that these elements are in place in order to build a teaching staff that is willing to go the distance and support the principal's leadership, in the best interest of the students.

DEALING WITH INEFFECTIVE TEACHERS

The expectation is: row with us or get out of the boat.
—Dr. Dana McCauley, National Distinguished Principal, Maryland

Take immediate steps to intervene when teachers are ineffective. Once the principal has witnessed a problem, he or she must counsel the teacher, provide support, offer new ways of doing things, and encourage the teacher to observe more effective peers and follow that model.

The principal should provide clear direction to an ineffective teacher to indicate: (a) there is a problem, (b) the principal is there to help with the problem, and (c) the principal expects the teacher to improve. If the problem is extreme, the principal may need to recommend that the teacher not continue as an educator unless positive change occurs.

> *I believe it is important for less effective teachers to be exposed to a variety of excellent instructors. Some teachers have just never seen good teaching. I believe most teachers want to be great teachers. . . . Sometimes teachers need to see what is being done and understand what good teaching looks like.*
> —Dr. Michael P. Lucas, National Blue Ribbon School Principal,
> Pennsylvania

Unless they receive information to the contrary, most people think they are doing a good job. It is the role of the principal to change this perception when teachers are not performing in a way that promotes and increases student achievement. Principals do this by being clear and direct with teachers who are not performing to expectations.

Principals who are direct and communicate well about their concerns for a teacher's performance may see measurable improvement—simply based on the fact that the problem has been made evident to the teacher. Most teachers want to do a good job. Given the information and support they need to make a positive change, most will endeavor to become better at their work. Mentoring, guidance, and the opportunity to observe other good teachers may contribute to an underperforming teacher's potential for success.

> *Improve their weaknesses. If it is instruction, we focus on that. What has helped me is to identify their weaknesses and have them work with people who have strengths in those areas.*
> —Kelly Wilmore, National Blue Ribbon School Principal, Virginia

There are ineffective teachers who will not improve, despite a principal's best efforts. This group usually consists of people who lack the basic skills for teaching, or people who are not motivated to do the job well.

Some teachers may try very hard, but simply are not effective in connecting with children. These teachers may take copious notes during their meetings with the principal, put in many hours trying to improve, and spend time consulting with colleagues, but still are incapable of effective teaching. These may prove to be the hardest staff members for a principal to correct or discipline, because their hearts are in the right place—they simply lack inherent talent for the job. Just as we are not all built to be football players, not everyone has the talent to teach. It is as simple as that.

Other ineffective teachers have the skills to teach but lack the interest, dedication, or impetus to do a good job. Teachers who fall into this category would rather read their e-mail than teach, for example, or may arrive at work with the morning newspaper under their arm and run out of the door as soon as the school day ends. This type of teacher almost never improves, because he or she lacks the necessary motivation. Effective principals encourage these poor performers to leave the profession.

> *I have a philosophy that you don't get rid of people, you try to make them better first. So we work with them. I tell them one on one, "Either you pick it up, or I'm going to find someone who will."*
> —Kelly Wilmore, National Blue Ribbon School Principal, Virginia

THE IMPORTANCE OF TAKING ACTION

> *I have learned that the longer you wait the bigger price you pay if you fail to take action. You lose the respect of others in the building if you allow bad behavior to continue.*
> —Budd A. Dingwall, National Distinguished Principal, North Carolina

Once a principal has determined that a teacher has a problem, it does no good to wait to take action. Some school leaders, however, need to assure themselves that there is an issue by revisiting the situation several times before addressing it. They may go back to visit the classroom and observe lessons many times in order to be certain that their hunches are correct. Assured that there is a problem worthy of correction, a principal needs to gather up the courage to address the problem and determine how best to address it.

Waiting or failing to act will have several negative consequences. First, it will allow the teacher's poor practices to become ingrained as habits. If the principal has seen the teacher in action several times and failed to intervene, or said nothing, the teacher may assume he or she is doing a good job. Others who observe the poor performance of the teacher and the lack of action on the part of the principal may start to believe that this level of performance is acceptable, or at least allowed in the school setting.

I have had one or two people that have said, "Gosh that person is borderline." If you think they are borderline, you should probably let them go. It is not really better for them [to continue as teachers], and in many cases it won't work out.
— Sanford E. Nelson, National Distinguished Principal, Minnesota

How should the principal respond when a teacher's performance falls below expectations? There are many ways to intervene, but a few absolutes: be confidential, be respectful, be direct, and be expeditious.

- Maintain confidentiality by finding a place to talk with the teacher privately.
- Be respectful of the teacher's feelings. It is best to have the conversation at the end of the day, so that if the teacher is upset, he or she is not required to return to the students.
- Be direct and clear. The teacher should walk away from the conversation understanding the principal's concerns, what the teacher is expected to do about the issues, and the timeline or deadline for improvement.
- Do not delay. Nobody wants to confront bad teaching or poor behavior, but a principal does no one any good by waiting to have this kind of conversation. Identify what needs to be done, and confront the situation immediately.

If the principal thinks the teacher is going to be successful in achieving the necessary improvements, and simply needs some help, the best route is to talk with and coach the teacher toward improved performance. However, if after a verbal warning or two, or perhaps even three, the behavior continues or no improvement results, the principal will need to document the situation and put any habitual examples of poor teaching behavior in writing.

Stick to the facts. Say, "I noticed that on [date] you were not in your classroom when I walked by at 9 a.m. You came back five or six minutes later and said you had been running off some papers. We talked about the importance of being prepared. Then I noticed on [date] I stopped by your class and again you were not there. This appears to be a habit. What help do you need to get this to stop?" . . . You always set the next meeting time and expectations for follow-up when you have had more than just a warning or two or three. Here is our action plan. Here is what we'll be looking for. Help to solve the problem without taking over the problem.
— Budd A. Dingwall, National Distinguished Principal, North Carolina

*When it comes to documenting underperforming staff members, if it is not in
writing, it is as if it never happened.*
    —Dr. Deborah Collins, deputy superintendent, Monrovia, California

When a principal gets serious about documenting a teacher's poor
performance, in effect that staff member is being put on notice that he or
she may not be recommended to continue in this work. If there is a
chance—now or down the road—that the teacher will be asked not to
continue employment at the school, a principal should start documenting
the situation in writing.

Verbal corrections do not count in dismissal hearings because a principal cannot prove that such interactions took place. If a principal is serious
about taking action against a teacher, potentially including termination,
corrective action must be in writing. Keep a detailed file and be orderly
with documentation of unacceptable or subpar teaching performance.
This paperwork will serve well in the event that the employee is asked
not to continue.

*Holding someone accountable and giving them a timeline works great for me. I
do it immediately. I don't waste a second.*
    —Lucille Keaton, National Distinguished Principal, Nevada

How many times should a principal talk with an underperforming
teacher about the undesired behavior or difficult issue? What is considered fair warning?

The short answer is: it depends. If a teacher has a minor infraction,
such as a habit of arriving five minutes late in the morning during a time
when students are being supervised by others, a principal may give two
or three verbal reminders before leaving a note in the employee's mailbox
or moving further up the progression of employee discipline.

If, however, the infraction is more serious, the principal may opt to
write an immediate letter of reprimand. For example, if a teacher walks
away from a class of five-year-olds, leaving them unattended in the classroom, the severity of such behavior is a guiding factor in the principal's
response. Behavior that threatens student safety and is a potential liabil-
ity to the school requires immediate documentation.

A principal may weigh all factors in determining how many times to
warn verbally before beginning to document a problem. In no case, however, should the principal remind an employee of a performance problem
more than three times before putting the issue into writing. Samples of
disciplinary letters are located in the appendix.

Most teachers want to be good at what they do. The ones hurting kids and providing poor instruction need to be dealt with swiftly. They are not interested in improving. I have had success in riding them out by visiting their classrooms daily and holding them to a higher standard than they prefer. Fortunately for me, I have a majority of excellent teachers in our staff.

—Anonymous study participant

UNCOMFORTABLE CONVERSATIONS

Be thoughtful. Couch the conversation in the confidence they can improve. . . . Acknowledge areas of strength. . . . Outline what [you] are going to do to assist the person. Recognize that when they walk out they are going to be really upset.

—Michael E. Friel, National Distinguished Principal, Lebanon

There is an art to "the uncomfortable conversation." A principal who finds that it takes courage to talk with a staff member about something so important that it must be said despite discomfort is about to engage in an uncomfortable conversation. This type of conversation is not merely corrective; it may be a career-changing discussion for the teacher.

There are at least two elements to such a discussion: the principal makes it clear there is a very big problem to address, and the principal sets out the expectation that the staff member will make improvements or risk disciplinary action.

A principal may discover many ways to approach such conversations with underperforming staff, but all involve preparation and forethought. Here are guidelines a principal may wish to follow.

First, the principal should ensure that the conversation occurs in a private place.

Second, depending on the seriousness of the offense, the principal may wish to have a witness present, and the staff member should be allowed to bring someone to observe the meeting as well. In that case, the principal should inform the employee of the opportunity to bring an observer to the meeting and the employee should be given adequate time to make arrangements for that person to be present. That said, the principal should not allow the teacher to delay the conference or avoid a meeting with the commonly used excuse, "I can't arrange for a representative."

Third, the principal should be sure the employee understands in advance that this will be a serious discussion. The principal may wish to say directly, "This is going to be a difficult conversation," when arranging the meeting. Knowing that they are walking into a challenging set of circumstances will help employees mentally prepare for what they are about to hear.

> *You rehearse over and over. Have a witness with you. I try to say as little as possible. . . . You simply say, "Your gifts do not meet our needs." That's a way that shows respect for the human being. "You have talents, just not what we need at this school at this time."*
>
> —Sister Marie Blanchette, National Blue Ribbon School Principal,
> Tennessee

Fourth, a principal should think ahead about what to say. Many principals like to write their thoughts down on paper ahead of time. Clarity in the message increases the likelihood the message will be understood by the employee. This will help the conversation meet its intended goal of communicating the deficit or issue and seeking correction. A principal should say what needs to be said in direct, clear terms and as honestly and kindly as possible—and then end the meeting.

Fifth, the principal should not make it a long meeting, or mix the corrective discussion in with other items of business. In part this is because usually the employee will be upset. Some people will flee after receiving bad news, some will cry, and some will be angry. Still others will appear to be out of touch with the severity of the situation. Regardless of how an employee reacts, nobody will benefit from a long meeting and the principal cannot make the situation better by over-talking.

> *If you are honest and up front, not having anger in your voice, then I think people in the end say, "I don't like what happened," but that doesn't mean I don't like the person.*
>
> —Sanford E. Nelson, National Distinguished Principal, Minnesota

DISCIPLINARY LETTERS

A letter of reprimand is a formal letter documenting an event, series of events, or habitual undesired behavior of an employee. Writing a letter of reprimand is a serious step for a principal to take, and usually follows multiple verbal corrections, coaching, support, and teacher training. A letter of reprimand can, however, be written immediately when an employee has made an egregious violation of the rules or has put students in an unsafe situation.

> *Honesty is the best policy. Teachers who are not succeeding know it and are not happy. Sometimes, it's the wrong mix. Sometimes, it's the wrong profession.*
>
> —Dr. Angel J. Barrett, National Distinguished Principal, California

The contents of written reprimands vary. Here is one of many possible outlines to follow in writing such a document:

- Describe the problem. Include in this statement the rule, policy, or law that the employee violated.
- Explain the effect of the employee's behavior on others, especially as it relates to students, staff, school safety, or parent perceptions.
- Spell out in explicit terms the changes the principal expects to see for improvement of the employee's behavior.
- Offer support in helping the employee to improve.
- Provide a timeline by which changes are expected to take place, and a date on which the principal will revisit the issue with the employee to check for improvement.

Begin a letter of reprimand by outlining the problem, as in the following example:

> Mrs. Jones, on April 10, I walked by your classroom at 10 a.m. and found your class unattended. The students were running around the room and playing with one other. Some students were practicing karate moves on each other. I found you next door, talking with Mr. Hernandez about the party on Friday. As you recall, a similar incident occurred on March 8 and again on March 24. On both prior occasions I spoke with you about this behavior, and on March 24 you received a written letter of reprimand for the incidents.

Next, draw a connection between the employee's undesired behavior and the effect of that behavior on students, staff, or the school as a whole. This section should answer the question, "So what?" For example: "When you leave your class unattended, it impacts the students in your class because it threatens their safety. When you are absent, no adult is ensuring that they do not cause harm to themselves or others."

The letter should tell the employee of the principal's expectation for changes in behavior. This section of the letter should be direct and written very clearly. For example:

> Effective immediately, you are directed to maintain close supervision of your class when students are under your care. Specifically, you are to remain in the same room with them or within twenty feet of your students when they are not in your classroom. You are to maintain full visual contact with your students when they are under your supervision.

Next, offer a statement of support that will be helpful in curbing the employee's bad behavior. For example:

> In order to assist you in better understanding appropriate supervision of students, you are to watch a video series about effective strategies for appropriate student supervision in the classroom setting. Also, I have arranged for you to observe Mrs. Brown's class, and then scheduled a time for you to talk with her about the strategies she uses to provide appropriate oversight of her class. Release time will be provided for this classroom visit. When we meet to review your progress in improving classroom oversight, I will ask you about these two learning experiences and I will be prepared to answer any questions you have that may arise from these experiences.

Conclude the letter by outlining a timeline for improvement. For example:

> An immediate change in your supervision of your students is expected. I plan to revisit this issue in a meeting with you on May 3 at 2 p.m. in my office. By that time, I expect you to have accomplished the above-mentioned steps. It is my expectation that henceforward, appropriate supervision will no longer be an issue in your classroom.

Letters of reprimand may seem brusque or abrupt, but their purpose is to be clear in the statement of the problem, expectations for employee improvement, and a timeline for improvement. Such letters should avoid wordiness, state exactly what the person should do differently, and clearly tell the employee about expectations for changes in behavior. A sample disciplinary letter can be found in the appendix.

IMPROVEMENT PLANS

When the principal realizes that a staff member may not be recommended for continued employment, it is fair to create an improvement plan that should be issued to the employee at least four months (preferably six) before the date that employment would be terminated.

> *I don't hesitate to do a plan of improvement to give [teachers] a chance to improve or leave the profession. My less effective teachers chose to leave. We don't push them off to another school. We don't shield an employee from the truth to get them out of the building and into someone else's.*
> —Bruce E. Reynolds, National Distinguished Principal, Oregon

There is a difference between a letter of reprimand and an improvement plan. The letter of reprimand documents one or more incidents of misconduct. A letter of reprimand may be used for a major isolated incident, particularly when the health or safety of students is threatened. Such a letter also may be used to precede an improvement plan for an employee with a history of poor performance.

An improvement plan is similar to a letter of reprimand, except that it also shows long-term intent to work with an employee to improve performance. It may be written for situations that are not urgent—for example, those that do not relate to student health and safety, but involve long-term issues that must be addressed such as timeliness, orderliness, or effectiveness. An improvement plan may be written for an employee who has not had any egregious disciplinary issue, but simply is not teaching effectively.

It is appropriate to issue an improvement plan for any employee that the principal intends not to recommend for re-employment. A good rule of thumb is to provide the employee with at least six months' advance notice in the form of an improvement plan, in order to inform the person that there is a serious issue with their performance that must be addressed, prior to a principal's action to terminate the employee. This form of intervention and corrective action is a fair way to ensure that the employee has a clear understanding of the perceived shortcomings, as well as time to attempt to fix them prior to termination.

While improvement plans can vary, following are steps principals may take in creating such a document:

- Outline the problem. Explain what the employee is doing that is unsatisfactory.

- Tell how this behavior or actions negatively affect others, such as students, staff, or the school as a whole. Clearly make a connection between the employee's poor performance and the results for students.
- State the improvements the principal wishes to see in the performance of the employee.
- Outline a long-term plan for improvement. This is the step that makes an improvement plan different from a letter of reprimand.
- Provide a timeline by which expected changes are to be made by the employee. Specify the date, time, and place at which the principal will meet with the employee to revisit the issue.

Here is a skeleton of an improvement plan.

First, explain the problem: "Mrs. Jones, when you use a loud, abrasive tone of voice with your students, they perceive you are angry with them. This tone of voice pervades your teaching, and frightens your students."

Explain the impact: "Children who are afraid do not learn as effectively as possible. They also go home and tell their parents that the teacher is yelling at them. Parents complain and want to take their children out of your class."

Describe improvements the principal expects to see: "Effective immediately, you are directed to use a softer, gentler tone of voice with your kindergarteners."

Spell out the plan for improvement. For example:

> Changing the tone of voice you use in teaching will take effort on your part. In order to assist you, I will provide the following support mechanisms: (1) A decibel meter. This meter flashes red when the decibels of the speaker or classroom exceed a given level. Use this as a guide for the loudness of your voice. (2) Our speech teacher will work with you to help you learn to monitor your tone of voice, both on a weekly one-on-one basis, and in a weekly classroom visit. (3) I will meet with you monthly to talk with you about your perceptions of improvement of this issue, to share the feedback I have received from parents, and to provide you with my observations of changes made in the tone you use while communicating with students in your classroom.

Finally, provide a timeline: "On [date, time, and place] I will meet with you to revisit this issue. If you are unable to correct the tone you are using with your kindergarteners, you may be reassigned to another grade level. We will discuss this possibility further when we meet at the end of this improvement period."

A sample improvement plan is in the appendix. If a principal anticipates terminating an employee within a year, it is appropriate to write an improvement plan. The improvement plan documents efforts the principal has made to help the employee improve, and is important in proving that the principal has attempted to provide support in correcting the behavior of the teacher.

FIRING PERSONNEL

Rule 1: Be absolutely sure there is sufficient cause and documentation. Rule 2: Be sure all policies and procedures are being followed. Rule 3: Keep the director of personnel informed about the process. Rule 4: Do not discuss the situation with other staff members. Rule 5: If there is sufficient cause, do not second-guess the necessary decision.
—Dr. Jane Koberlein, National Distinguished Principal, Missouri

If underperforming teachers are in their probationary or non-permanent years, the principal owes it to the students and staff, and to this new teacher, to take action to either correct the problem or discontinue employment of the teacher. If the principal has any doubts about a new teacher, it is far better to terminate employment rather than retain the teacher and grant them permanent status in the school system.

When in doubt, send them out.

—Anonymous

In the public sector, a principal's chances of having the resources, power, authority, and wherewithal to terminate employment of a tenured staff member are slim. A principal may, through strong relationship building, be able to counsel an underperforming teacher out of the profession or seek other kind but direct ways to encourage such a teacher to move on to a profession more suited to his or her skills.

Effective principals make sure of several actions if they are serious about removing a permanent teacher from employment. First, they make absolutely sure they have a good case, and sufficient documentation. A principal should study the situation judiciously. If he or she is unsure whether to recommend the teacher for continued employment, it is best to consult with the school district central office frequently over a period of time about the situation.

The principal should also watch the teacher carefully. If a teacher is ineffective enough to be recommended for termination, the employee will display repeated patterns of misconduct or poor teaching behaviors. It does not pay to rush into personnel actions against permanent teachers without taking the time for careful documentation and communication with the district's personnel office.

The principal must ensure that all applicable policies and procedures have been followed and should check the documentation before taking action against a permanent employee. Is the principal's case sound, thorough, complete, dated, well organized, and well reasoned? Has a pattern of poor employee behavior been thoroughly established and documented? Has the principal followed the district's guidelines, protocols, and procedures, and remained within the requirements of the collective bargaining agreement if the employee is part of a union? If the answer to any of these questions is "No," the principal should continue to document the case.

The paperwork and documentation of poor employee performance must be impeccable in order to prevail in a termination case.

Keep the director of personnel informed. If a principal has documentation in place concerning a poor-performing teacher, the appropriate personnel official at the district level should be informed and the principal should review the situation with the personnel official. That person doubtless will have questions, and will want to see past observations and other forms of documentation of the employee's problem.

A personnel director who thinks that a principal is correct in asserting that an employee should be terminated often will seek legal counsel to gather another opinion in the matter. This is a normal protocol for a termination proceeding.

The situation should not be discussed with other staff members. As a principal goes through the long, difficult process to terminate a teacher's employment, it is natural to want to share stories and facts about the case with others. The principal must strenuously resist this temptation, however. Such situations must be absolutely confidential.

> You may in your heart know that this person needs to get out of the profession. You have done what you can. . . . But if your district is not in your corner, you are going to be the one in the fire, not the teacher. Before you go down that

road that gets dark and ugly, be sure that the district office is in your corner
and you are not left hanging in the wind.
—Study participant, name intentionally omitted

Despite hours of preparation, endless paperwork, and difficult meetings, if the central office of the school district does not support the assertion that an employee should be let go, the principal will need to accept this fact. Many become impassioned about "the principle of the matter" when it comes to employees who have a negative effect on students, but the district officials may more fully understand the other costs associated with a termination case and back away.

It is not uncommon for a teacher termination case to cost the district legal fees in the range of double the teacher's annual salary. If the district is not willing to spend these funds to take legal action against a teacher, the principal should advocate for other options. For example, can the teacher be put on day-to-day substitute status? Could the teacher be assigned to shelve books in the library, run a small group for student enrichment, or spend days filing? Most of the time, steps such as these would be considered demotions and may not be allowable, and could end up as legal matters to be investigated with the central office and legal counsel. Creativity in these situations, however, can sometimes lead to alternatives that produce the needed results for all parties.

Even if a district may choose not to support the termination of a teacher's employment, most central office administrators will take steps to find solutions that improve the situation in order to benefit students.

Don't be afraid to admit that you made a mistake, and correct the mistake by
moving the person on, even if it takes many legal battles, sleepless nights.
—Dr. Paul M. Schley, National Blue Ribbon School Principal,
Wisconsin

If there is sufficient cause, however hard disciplinary action may be, a principal should not hesitate to bring about change. Taking disciplinary action against teachers, reprimanding them, or recommending them for termination can be excruciatingly difficult and very hard work. It can also be heart wrenching, especially when an employee who is trying hard simply cannot do the job.

The principal should remember, however, that the object of education is to serve the students first and foremost, not the teachers. It is important to ask, "What is best for the children?" If a principal finds that he or she is spending a lot of time wrestling with the negative impact of a particular teacher, applying this filter will quickly help make the decision to pursue the employee's termination for the long-term benefits to the children.

STAND AGAINST TRANSFERRING POORLY PERFORMING TEACHERS

I have tried hard to work with less effective teachers. However, those who have refused to follow letters of directives or professional development plans have transferred to other schools. I do not let any other principal get surprised by their lack of initiative. I do not believe in allowing them to become someone else's problem. I inform those principals what we have done and if he or she still chooses to hire the person, at least I know in my heart I was professionally honest and truthful.

—Dr. Jolie D. Hardin, National Distinguished Principal, Georgia

Educators serve all students. It does nobody any good to allow a poor teacher to transfer to another school, where they will negatively impact other children in a different environment. Some call this "the dance of the lemons."

Stand firmly against allowing poorly performing employees to transfer from site to site. If a principal knows such an employee is seeking a transfer, it is that principal's responsibility to tell the receiving principal their perceptions of the poorly performing teacher's work, and try to impede the transfer as something that will have negative long-term results for students.

When poorly performing teachers are allowed to transfer to another site, the work that has been done to help them improve is erased, and they begin anew with a principal who must learn their areas of weakness before engaging in improvement efforts. This action, while giving poorly performing teachers a fresh start, merely moves their performance issues to a new site, where this teacher negatively impacts a new set of students.

Rather than encouraging a teacher to transfer, which is the easier route for a principal, instead take action to correct the problem. If a staff person is ineffective, encourage him or her to move to another profession or a different role for which the person is better suited.

SUMMARY

Working with teachers to make continuous improvement in teaching and learning is the most important role of the school principal. It has a direct effect on improvement efforts and increases in student achievement.

In daily work, the principal should support teachers who are leading the charge for improvement and change.

The principal should observe, counsel, and support all teachers, but when an underperforming teacher does not yet have permanent status, the principal should not hesitate to discontinue that teacher's employment. A principal should take formal steps to document teachers who are deemed to be ineffective with students, seeking solutions that may include termination if appropriate.

Implications for Action

- The principal's most important work is selecting, supporting, coaching, and training the instructional team at the school. A principal must take this role seriously, devoting the greatest portion of his or her time, effort, and support to positive, successful staff members.
- A principal should be careful and cautious in hiring. Check references and read personnel files carefully.
- In order to retain positive people at the school, a principal needs to help staff be comfortable, feel rewarded, grow professionally, and feel safe at work.
- When a principal determines that a teacher is not effective, clear and prompt action should be taken. If the behavior issue is a serious one, the principal should document the situation in writing and put the teacher on notice that he or she must improve or face disciplinary action.
- The principal must be willing to take on uncomfortable conversations with underperforming staff. The work of improving the behavior and performance of teachers is critically important to a principal's efforts to improve student achievement.
- If a principal has serious concerns about an employee's performance, an improvement plan should be created. The plan should make the concerns clear to the employee and document them for the record.

- An effective principal has the courage to pursue termination for teachers who fail to positively impact student achievement. The principal may or may not be successful in teacher termination efforts, but it is a moral obligation to reduce a poorly performing teacher's effect on students and student achievement.

- A good principal does not allow poorly performing teachers from one school site to be transferred to another site without the receiving principal understanding the concerns about the teacher. The principal understands and cares about how such transfers negatively affect children at the receiving school.

A STORY FROM THE FIELD

Told by Linda K. Wagner (author of this book)

James* was a twelve-year-old student in an intensive class for students with extreme physical limitations. He had an amazing smile and what appeared to be an optimistic spirit. His body was so misshapen and his verbal skills so limited, however, that the adults in his life believed his mental abilities to be extremely limited as well.

James had the good fortune of having a very perceptive and talented teacher. Over time and through a great deal of creativity, his teacher found ways to communicate with him. She realized that James was not only of normal cognition, but actually quite bright. With a great deal of catch-up work and the help of devices to assist his speech, his teacher thought he might eventually be able to attend regular classes.

In order to obtain the services James needed, his teacher knew she would have to shatter the opinions held by the adults in James's life, including James's own parents. I have rarely seen a teacher advocate so adamantly on behalf of a child. Little by little, James and his teacher demonstrated to caregivers and other adults that James was capable of much more than the intensive class program had been offering.

By the time James left our school, he was attending regular classes in his walker with the help of an aide. A device had been provided to him to allow him to push buttons that would spell words. This became his communication system. With his warm, friendly smile, even though he could not speak with the adults and children at the school, James became a beloved member of the student body. When he graduated, we all cried. Despite his limitations, James achieved beyond our wildest dreams.

*The student's name in this story has been changed for privacy.

SIX

Encouraging Site-Based Leadership

When principals empower teachers, they create a strong staff not dependent upon a few leaders, but many who have an area of expertise worthy of sharing.
—Dr. Joann Borchetta, National Distinguished Principal, Connecticut

Effective principals know that in order to create improvements in instructional practices, they must begin with a strong, solid foundation: a good working relationship with teachers. Effective principals take the time and make the effort to not only work with their teachers but also get to know them as individuals.

Principals should be attuned to what is happening in the lives of the staff members. Good principals become aware of the interests and challenges of teachers and know what they most enjoy about their work. Principals who hope to foster positive relationships with staff members talk with their staff frequently, listen attentively, and provide help when possible.

I think one of the things that has helped me to win over my teachers right from the beginning, even when I didn't know them very well, was a handshake and a hug. Because we are a team, I am all about warm fuzzies. . . . I like to let them know that I am firm in what I believe in . . . but it is not my way or the highway. I need to know what they are thinking. Sometimes they have a better perspective on things and I need to hear from them. The better informed I am, the better decisions I can make.
—Cynthia L. Rodriguez, National Blue Ribbon School Principal, Texas

71

Listening to teachers, hearing their perspectives, and getting to know them as individuals helps to build relationships and ultimately improves the team.

> *One of the teachers said, "I don't want you to ask my opinion, I want you to tell me what to do and I'll do it." I said, "I know this is going to be hard for you, but I'm not going to do that. Once we do that, if it fails, then there is no ownership for you. If we decide together, we will both be involved in trying to make it better."*
>
> —Sanford E. Nelson, National Distinguished Principal, Minnesota

There are certain choices principals must make. Usually they are the tougher calls—the decisions that will be met with resistance by staff, students, parents, or the central office. In these cases, it is the role of the principal to stand up and make the decision on behalf of the school. These decisions may include firing employees who are not effective, moving teachers from one grade level to another, or expelling a student who has behaved poorly.

Most other judgment calls, however—nearly all instructional decisions and most decisions that impact staff—should be made with the input of the teachers or a smaller subset of the staff such as a leadership team. Teachers should be involved in such decisions as how the master schedule should be constructed, what subjects are taught at various points during the day, and the design of school-wide discipline plans.

Choices made and supported by the faculty will be more likely to have the buy-in of the teachers than those made by the principal alone. Decisions that directly affect teachers and their classrooms are best made with significant staff input, whenever possible.

> *Faculty members are active participants in decisions that impact and shape school climate, curriculum, and student achievement. . . . This . . . allows for a two-way flow of ideas, opinions, questions, concerns, and recommendations. I function as the leaven, and sometimes the glue, to keep all informed, grounded, focused, and responsive to student needs.*
>
> —Dr. Jane Koberlein, National Distinguished Principal, Missouri

Shared leadership helps principals to get their most important work done. Those teachers who lead other teachers tend to become increasingly positive, helpful, outgoing, and effective in their impact on the school campus.

> *I've heard many people say that they've worked hard at other schools, but when they come to this school, they feel the pressure (in a positive way). That*

is a well-oiled machine. People know what to teach and the best practices that make that possible. I've had several brand-new people come here and say, "I've had to rethink what I do," because it is obvious that the staff have high expectations of each other in addition to what the administration expects.

  —Brian M. Hull, National Distinguished Principal, Virginia

Leadership by teachers is central to student and school success. To involve the faculty at high levels of leadership, the principal should focus the spotlight on the top-performing teachers. Teachers who are participating actively in the work of the school, who have great attitudes, and who are making gains with their students lead by example. Teacher leadership may permeate the school building and becomes contagious when the principal supports and encourages teachers to lead their peers. Therefore, a majority of the principal's time is best spent with the "go-getters" among the teachers.

We take our best teachers and that's who we go with. Instead of fighting the people who don't want to be there . . . we focus on the leaders, and then everyone goes with it because the others don't want to be left behind.

  —Sammy Jackson, National Blue Ribbon School Principal, Oklahoma

Empower the teachers. Hire the best teachers and then let go. If they are the experts in the classroom, then I should not be micromanaging them or telling them "No" all the time. If you tell them "No" too often, they shut down.

  —Sister Marie Blanchette, National Blue Ribbon School Principal,
                     Tennessee

My team is made up of leaders within the building. They are my "go-to" people. I use them to get information out to the rest of the community. The team has evolved over time. I did not come in with any notions about who might be a part of that. It is not always positive people. I have learned that you may need people who see the other side of the coin or may not be the "yes" people.

  —Jill Flanders, National Distinguished Principal, Massachusetts

Most principals can find effective teacher leaders from among their staff members. In part this is done by examining who at the school site supports school-wide initiatives, both with their actions and their communication with other teachers.

Teachers who implement school-wide efforts with enthusiasm, are willing to teach their peers new concepts, and are role models for others in the learning process, are already leading the staff. Look for teachers who are well received by their peers and communicate effectively. A combination of positivity toward school-wide efforts and an existing rapport with other teachers can help teacher leaders to achieve great success in their work.

> *I want to be able to take my days off and know the school is in good hands. We have a lot of people in those roles. You have to see who wants to take it on. There are a lot who would look at it and say, "No way, that is not for me." There are only a few who have the personality type and desire to move into that type of leadership role. They have to be strong, and at the same time they need to love children. I look for people who love children, whom my students are comfortable with, who would be deemed by the kids at this school as fair. If you can find that person, they just thrive.*
>
> —Beth M. York, National Blue Ribbon School Principal, Tennessee

The principal should begin delegating leadership by asking staff members to take on small leadership tasks. For example, a principal may ask teachers who have leadership potential to help train new staff members. Or teachers who are suited to pick up leadership roles may be asked to supervise a club on campus or recruited to oversee a new curricular initiative. Over time, this core group of teacher leaders will reinforce school-wide efforts and help the principal move the school toward improved success.

> *I encourage leadership through delegation and empowerment. I look for those who have leadership qualities and I invest time in them, attempting to develop them.*
>
> —John-Mark Cain, National Blue Ribbon School Principal, Mississippi

SUMMARY

Effective principals realize that they cannot lead the school alone. It takes a team to do the important work of making significant changes happen in the best interest of students. Such principals select the most motivated teachers as teacher leaders. Those teachers are often the ones already involved in school-wide initiatives and who demonstrate dedication to the team. The principal should focus time and effort on these teachers, and encourage them to lead others. Leave a legacy of leadership at your school site by encouraging teachers to seek leadership opportunities and administrative training.

Implications for Action

- Recognize that you are only as good as the people who work for you. Hire well, train effectively, and encourage leadership.
- Focus on getting to know teachers as individuals. Relationships with staff build the employees' commitment to the organization.
- Encourage and promote teachers who support school-wide initiatives.
- Demonstrate to the school that the principal trusts and believes in the effectiveness of the teachers to teach and to positively impact the students and the whole school.
- When possible, include teachers in decision making related to instruction.

A STORY FROM THE FIELD

Told by Bruce Reynolds, National Distinguished Principal, Oregon

One of the kids that came to our school had a thick file. He was not successful academically. He had behavioral difficulties, and his parents were wary of the school. He had alienated himself from his peers, but was likable to us.

My team "circled the wagons." We looked for ways to be proactive, to help him with his peers and with academic success. We created opportunities in which he could be successful.

My team made a point of being welcoming to his parents. We visited with them when they came to school, and communicated successes and concerns.

By the end of the year his demeanor had changed. We were sorry to see him move on. Last year, he graduated from high school. We all got invitations and a note that said, "Thanks for seeing something in me that I didn't see in myself."

SEVEN

Making Parents a Part of the Team

The greatest tribute that I recall was a seventh grader whose parent, at his bar mitzvah, said, "You have been raised by a committee: the school, your grandparents, and your parents have all been an important part of your life." We want to be active partners in the learning and growing of our students.
—Andrew Polsky, National Blue Ribbon School Principal, California

Parents can be the most important teachers in a child's life if they are equipped with the tools they need to make a positive educational impact. Effective principals know this, and find ways to make parents—of all abilities and educational levels—active partners in the education of their children.

Partnering with parents begins with strong, consistent, and clear communication. Messages sent from the school to students' homes should help parents work with the school in meaningful ways. Frequent conversations between staff members and parents as well as messages, flyers, and newsletters from the school can help parents to feel like part of the solution and part of their child's educational team.

There are many ways to reach out to parents. From the traditional marquee in front of the school announcing major events to a newsletter sent home in each student's backpack, schools should make efforts to ensure that parents know about school programs and events.

Schools are finding less expensive, technology-based communication tools—for example, all-call telephone systems that allow schools to place automated calls to all parents. At other schools, text messages or other Internet-based messaging technology is designed to reach parents efficiently via computer or phone. Schools also are using blogs, e-mail, web-sites, and similar electronic tools to communicate information to parents.

> *We have gotten into Facebook. Parents like that. We have our own Twitter stream as well. A lot of schools have all-call systems. We do too, but we also have e-mail and texts. This goes out on a system similar to the all-call. Parents love it. It is quick, short, and to the point. When you can pop a text and parents can look at it really quickly, we've found that parents are more likely to participate in events.*
>
> —Sammy Jackson, National Blue Ribbon School Principal, Oklahoma

> *We give parents little magnets that have the school information. It is all on a little business card: the teachers' and principal's contact information, the teachers' conference periods, the direct phone line to the teachers, school hours, the fax number for the school, and the phone for the school.*
>
> —Cynthia L. Rodriguez, National Blue Ribbon School Principal, Texas

Parents should be invited to the school often and be encouraged to participate in school-wide events. From Back-to-School Night to awards ceremonies, to the science fair, to the volunteer tea, effective principals create a year-long plan that brings parents back to school over and over in an attempt to ensure that they are a part of their child's educational experience.

Much more personal than the messages that are sent to all parents are the personal phone calls that teachers and administrators make about a particular child's progress. A wise principal does not wait for a negative interaction with a child to make a first call to parents. Instead, a principal should call parents about positive events in their child's education, whenever time and other priorities allow for such personal contacts, and encourage teachers to do the same.

> *We recognized kids if they were responsible, taking a responsible risk, being flexible thinkers, and more. I would call the parents and say, "Hey, we're going to recognize your child's great work in an assembly." It was such a big deal for the parents. Extended families came, parents came. It was one of the greatest things I created as principal. Every month I would make eight or nine phone calls that were positive.*
>
> —Michael E. Friel, National Distinguished Principal, Lebanon

Parent conferences are of critical importance at all grade levels. From kindergarten through high school, parents need to know how their child is performing in school. Recent technology adds whole new possibilities for connecting with parents, giving them the ability to check grades and assignments online and connect with teachers via e-mail.

Still, there is nothing like a face-to-face conversation about a student's performance. As students move toward high school, however, it becomes increasingly difficult to maintain meaningful contact with parents. This is still worth the effort. Thoughtful principals should communicate with parents often and effectively at all grade levels, and ensure that teachers do the same.

It is not uncommon for the students who are the hardest to reach academically to have parents who are the most difficult to connect with in meaningful ways. This may be due to a number of factors, including financial difficulties, language barriers, and other life struggles. Whatever the case, special attention should be paid to forging connections with hard-to-reach students and their parents.

> *We really needed buy-in from parents to make sure they were on board. Some [students] were attendance problems, some were kids who are home alone with parents working multiple jobs. . . . Once we assigned classes, we sat down with each teacher, all of whom had a small group of at-risk students. We set up an expectation in the building that all teachers will meet with the parents of all of these students in the first five or six weeks of school. . . . We came to agreements on what the parents would do at home, what we would do at school. . . . A plan was set up that encouraged buy-in [and the notion] that we are a team. We do that for every student who has not been doing well. We basically are tracking those students and watching them over a period of time and being sure they get the support they need.*
> —Brian M. Hull, National Distinguished Principal, Virginia

Schools should make overt efforts to assist parents whose children struggle the most. This can take many forms, but should begin with helping ease the parents' difficulties in communicating with the school. Translation across language barriers should be provided as appropriate, and steps taken to ensure that parents understand what is said to them about their children. Schools should assist with transportation difficulties that keep parents from getting to and from the school whenever possible.

Regardless of the inherent difficulties of this work, these efforts to communicate pay dividends as students and teachers learn that parents are partners in the work of education.

> *When they register, we ask them if they would be interested in being connected with someone in the PTA (Parent Teacher Association). If they say "Yes,"*

*someone who speaks their language calls and connects with them, and wel-
comes them to the site. With forty-six different languages spoken in our school,
we've developed a cadre of people representing different languages. We have
helped to train these volunteers to know about the school, know the expectations, and convey their knowledge of the culture. Now when we have events at
school, most cultures are represented. It has been a slow process, but an effective one.*

—Brian M. Hull, National Distinguished Principal, Virginia

SUMMARY

Parents are important partners in the education of children. The principal
should put in place overt actions to communicate with parents regularly,
keeping them apprised of school-wide efforts, events, and progress of the
child or children in the family. When things appear to be difficult for a
family, schools should be thoughtful in finding ways to bridge these
issues—for example, by helping parents with language barriers and crafting opportunities for parents to work successfully with the school. Working with parents is not always easy, but it is essential in order to secure
the academic progress of the children who benefit from these connections.

Implications for Action

- Parents should be partners in the education of their children. Regardless how difficult, a principal must go out of his or her way to
  foster good connections with parents.
- Principals should communicate with parents consistently and in
  multiple ways.
- A thoughtful principal provides parents with the time, space, and
  opportunity to help the school with the vital work of educating the
  child. When possible, a principal will find someone who can communicate with parents in their own language.
- A good principal is creative, and tries many different ways to reach
  parents until strong partnerships are forged, and the parents become important partners in the work of education.

A STORY FROM THE FIELD

Told by Jonathan A. Ross, National Distinguished Principal, Pennsylvania

I had a situation with a girl in sixth grade. She had an older sibling at the time. That tends to lead to girls knowing a lot of kids older than they are.

She was involved in a lot of unnecessary drama in her life, and was getting bullied a lot. She was hanging out with older kids and they were picking on her. She would take it personally. She was contributing, in a way, to the problems she had because of the choices she made.

I spent a lot of time with her during her sixth grade year. Her parents were antagonistic at first. They felt it was the school's problem. She was having a lot of crying and school-phobic type behaviors.

I gave it to her straight: here is what you did right, and here is what you did wrong. We made a connection.

Over three years at my site I saw improvement. When she left, her parents wrote me a note. They recognized that I helped her.

EIGHT

Working with the Central Office

Be a team player. When you get into a circumstance where you are thinking that what's going on is not supporting kids, don't be afraid to go about that issue in a way that builds relationships with those people.
—Sanford E. Nelson, National Distinguished Principal, Minnesota

Effective principals work in close collaboration with the central office of the school district. They understand that the central office is there to support their efforts and to make their work at the school site possible, although it may not always feel that way.

Principals report either directly or indirectly to a number of people at the central office. In the public sector, principals often are employed by a superintendent, who works with a school district board. In the private sector, commonly a board or group of individuals is responsible for school oversight.

Whatever the structure, principals may feel caught in the middle, with supervisors having authority over their work. A savvy principal, however, takes into consideration the opinions, desires, goals, and intentions of central office administrators and/or members of the school's governing board as he or she makes changes at the school level.

It is wise for a principal to maintain a close relationship with district administrators. Ways to maintain this relationship include checking in at the central office from time to time, walking through the office and greeting the staff who work there, making sure to return phone calls from headquarters promptly, and getting to know the central office support team as individuals. In return, central office staff will come to know and regard the principal as a partner in their work.

> *I smile, say "Hello," and call them by name. I do what I am asked to do and [meet] the deadlines that are given me. When support personnel have come to our building for maintenance or repair, I offer them chocolate or bottled water. They just want people to recognize them and appreciate them. I ask questions when I really do not know the answer, to [avoid] making silly mistakes.*
> —Rhonda M. Parmer, National Distinguished Principal, Texas

It is critical for principals to inform their supervisors of important events, occurrences, and issues at the school site. This allows the supervisor to make well-informed decisions. Principals should operate under the rule of "no surprises" when it comes to their relationship with the central office.

> *I always feel that the more information you give the district office the better. . . . When e-mailing or calling about something, I always operate under this theory: If I were in his position would I want to know the information or situation that I as the principal am dealing with? If the answer is "Yes," then I contact him, even if it is "telling" on myself for something that will never get to his level. I never want him to be surprised by something from my building.*
> —Jason Cameron , National Blue Ribbon School Principal, Delaware

Invite those who oversee district operations to visit the school. Walk them around the site, talk about programs, and educate them about important efforts or events. Central office administrators often have very busy schedules, but invitations from the principal will go a long way in making them feel that the principal wants to work with them and welcome them to the school site.

Welcome the superintendent and top-level staff members to your campus. Offer the superintendent the opportunity to walk around the site and keep him or her informed about the events, programs, news, and other happenings on the campus.

> *I am not a superintendent, and I don't always know all the reasons why things are done as they are. You try to help them to understand where you are coming from, and you try to understand where they are coming from.*
> —Sanford E. Nelson, National Distinguished Principal, Minnesota

There will be times when those with authority over the principal will impose changes that may not be perceived as beneficial. When this happens, the principal should inquire professionally, but privately, about the changes. A principal may opt to discuss, debate, and perhaps even negotiate the issue with a direct supervisor, depending on whether he or she feels able to be open about the concerns.

Whatever a principal chooses to say to a superior privately, behind closed doors, he or she should be careful what is said publicly. Because staff members and school constituents may be required to live with these changes, the principal should be careful not to speak ill of the required changes with the school staff.

In the event that a decision is made despite objections, the principal must find a way to support the decision. The principal works for administrators at the central office, and should not be perceived as undermining their authority. Staff members should see the principal and the central office show a unified front.

It is the principal's role to ensure that what she or he says to staff about changes is positive, despite actual feelings about the changes.

> *I made the decision that nobody would hear me complain. . . . While it was not personally best for me, I knew it would help the whole.*
> —Jonathan A. Ross, National Distinguished Principal, Pennsylvania

The central office has many pressures and requirements unknown to school sites. For example, personnel issues at other sites may, by necessity, affect the school. There will be fiscal constraints, facilities issues, and myriad other dilemmas which will have impacts felt at the site level. Board members will have goals they hope to see achieved during their time on the board, superintendents will have agendas for instructional change, and constituents will complain about one thing or another to administrators above the level of the principal. There may be many things happening at the central office level about which the principal is not even aware. The principal should keep this in mind in approaching work with the central office.

> *Going to bat head-to-head with the pitcher doesn't always work. Sometimes stealing second base is a better approach. You realize that what you are trying to do is going to require some public relations work with the central office. For example, Reading Recovery. We started small, talked it up with others. Our central office people were reluctant. So we had them come in and watch the individual impact on kids. They became our greatest advocates.*
> —Sanford E. Nelson, National Distinguished Principal, Minnesota

Be careful not to blindside the central office. When there is an issue of significance, the principal should call the central office and let them know. Principals who keep their supervisors apprised of things that are happening at the school site help administrators not only know the challenges and opportunities they face but also understand the impact of district decisions.

SUMMARY

The central office has the task of making the whole school system work. From time to time, this will mean administrators must ask things of a principal or school that may not be best for that site, but may help with a goal held by the larger school system. When such things happen, principals should voice their concerns in a private setting.

Principals also should be careful not to taint the perspectives of those at the school who will have to work with any new sets of circumstances that are imposed on them by the central office.

A principal should advocate diplomatically for his or her school site. To the extent possible, the principals must be supportive of the central office and attempt to understand decisions that administrators make. Then, if a decision stands despite the principal's opposition, he or she should be positive about it with staff.

It is best for principals to maintain strong, solid relationships with superiors and/or the school board, as well as with the individuals who serve the school from the central office level.

Implications for Action

- Principals may not like what they are asked to do by supervisors or administrators at a district or central office. If a principal questions what he or she has been asked to do, any concerns should be shared in a private conversation with a supervisor, and the conversation should be conducted with respect.
- Sometimes, school sites will be asked to help solve "big-picture" or system-wide issues and challenges faced by the entire school system.
- The central office staff is a key part of the team that helps a school to be successful. A wise principal establishes strong relationships with the central office staff.

A STORY FROM THE FIELD

Letter from a parent, received and shared by Dr. Christopher Kennedy, National Distinguished Principal, Rhode Island

Hello Dr. Kennedy. I am Raj,* Olok's father. I am writing this mail to express my profound respect and overwhelming indebtedness to you and your school for all the care, education, and bearing with my son. My son indeed needed help. Your school provided it bountifully and handled him so affectionately that such a hard transition from India to the US became so much smoother for him and for me and my wife too. Now as much as my son enjoys the ambience in your school, I stay more assured and obliged for the favors. The recent gift of $100 is proof that you care and I am limited by my linguistic skills to express accordingly what it means to me, to him, and to my family. Olok is happy and wants to buy things which I could not afford with my income. I will remember all the favors and will explain to him when he grows up and is in position to understand what all he received from you, your school, teacher, and USA. I stay amazed and overwhelmed. I thank you again on behalf of my son.

*The names in this story have been changed for privacy.

NINE
Managing Your Time

Bell to bell with students and teachers. During that time, whatever paperwork I do, I do after the bells. During the school time, that is when people need you.
—Jonathan A. Ross, National Distinguished Principal, Pennsylvania

EFFECTIVE PRINCIPALS ARE VISIBLE

Effective principals know the time they spend interacting with students and teachers is the most valuable time of their day. Visiting classrooms, supervising students at lunch, greeting parents, and listening to staff members is essential work.

The paper that lies on the principal's desk is primarily rooted in the past. Principals who want to make a difference for the future get out of their offices and spend time in the classrooms, where teaching and learning take place.

Every day, I take time to remember why I became an educator and find something to do that exemplifies those reasons. Maybe it's lunch with the children. Maybe it's a student conference to check in with their progress. But every day, amid the paperwork and phone calls, I do this for myself.
—Dr. Angel J. Barrett, National Distinguished Principal, California

My goal is always to be with kids. Each lunch hour that I am at school. I wander around the lunchroom with students. I want them to see me. I enjoy the time that I get to spend asking students about their families, their hobbies, their interests. When a staff member is unable to fulfill a recess or lunch duty assignment, I step in. Again, I want to be seen! I try to spend my available time in classrooms, observing teachers at what they do best. I am continually amazed at the level of instruction and learning that I see in our building each day.

—Jacqueline Meyer, National Distinguished Principal, Idaho

Principals who spend their school day out on the school grounds and in classrooms rather than allowing themselves to be trapped in the office can handle issues before they become problems. If supervising lunch, the principal may see a problem brewing between students before it becomes a fight. The principal who stops by a teacher's class may observe that she is overly stressed, and may be able to cover her class to give her a break and prevent a negative situation. Principals who attend to things as they happen by being present and visible may prevent larger problems down the road.

DEALING WITH PAPERWORK

If the principal is most effective when "out and about" on the school campus, how does she or he keep up with the paperwork, mail, and e-mail that flood the office every day? Our study participants had several suggestions:

Deal with mail and e-mail quickly. Sort through mail and discard what is not needed, pass on what will be delegated, deal with the quick items, and have one small pile for larger projects. It is amazing how quickly mail can pile up on your desk and make finding things take so much time! The same goes with e-mail. Delete what you can, have folders for what you need to save, deal with what you can, and leave the small remainder in your inbox so you remember to take care of it as soon as you can.

—Paul Schley, National Blue Ribbon School Principal, Wisconsin

To deal with paperwork and correspondence, pick a given time each day during which there are few distractions. This may be before school starts, during a time in the academic day when less critical instruction is taking place, or after the students have gone home. At that time, the principal should close the door of his or her office and focus attention on moving rapidly through paperwork.

Sorting and eliminating paperwork daily will keep it from piling up and becoming a distraction to the principal's most important work, which is being present in the school and focusing on instruction.

Principals may get caught up in the notion of having an "open-door policy," thinking it means their door constantly needs to be open. Instead, create an "open-door policy" that means the principal is available at specified times during the day for staff members who need to speak with their leader. The principal should be available to staff at given times during the day, but should also find other quiet times to close the office door and take care of paperwork. This practice avoids the distractions that happen when staff members find a constantly open door leading to the principal's office.

KNOWING WHEN TO SAY "ENOUGH IS ENOUGH"

The work of the principal is never done. A school leader could spend every waking hour dedicated to the work of the school—but this approach will exhaust even the most energetic principal.

A principal should put in a solid work day of at least eight hours, and no more than twelve, and then go home. Whatever did not get done in that period of time will wait for another day. Managing the length of the work day will allow a principal to get enough rest at home and remain ready for the difficult job of school leadership.

A principal also should make rules about work and personal time and maintain these boundaries. The principal should expect to have only one or two work-related evening events per week. A principal who ends up with more than two evening obligations in a week should either seek someone else to supervise the extra events or stop planning so many events. Students, staff, and constituents need a happy, healthy principal, and managing the number of events slated to occur outside the school day is one way to achieve this goal.

Weekends may threaten to drain a principal's energy as well. Effective principals plan to be involved in school-related activities only one weekend day per month. If the principal is doing school-related business on more than one weekend a month, consider this excessive and find a way to curtail the additional activity or find substitute leaders who can stand in for the principal.

Good principals find ways to seek help in the oversight of extracurricular or evening and weekend events so that the school calendar does not run them ragged. A well-rested principal will serve the school far better than one who spends all available time and energy at the school and then has nothing left for family and friends.

SUMMARY

The principal should be visible, on the school grounds, and in classrooms whenever possible throughout the student day. Paperwork is optimally accomplished after students are gone for the day, or at other noncritical moments.

An effective principal takes care of him- or herself and does not to work so many evening and weekend events that he or she is exhausted and too tired to perform the important work of improving instruction. When faced with too many evening or weekend events, it is appropriate to seek substitute administrators or to curtail events that cause the principal to work excessive hours.

Implications for Action

- Be visible on campus, in classrooms, on the grounds, and in the cafeteria throughout the school day. The principal's presence keeps expectations high for students and staff, and can forestall problems or keep negative behavior from spiraling out of control.
- The principal sets intentional times to do paperwork, at moments that are not instructionally significant, preferably when students are not on campus.
- A healthy principal guards personal time in order to maintain a balanced personal and professional life, as well as energy for the job. It is acceptable to plan fewer events or use substitute administrators in order to grant the principal needed rest during evenings and weekends.

A STORY FROM THE FIELD

Told by Dr. Angel J. Barrett, National Distinguished Principal, California

When I was two years old, my parents were told that my father would not live until I was a teenager. When I was in fourth grade, he was in the hospital most of the time. My mother stayed at the hospital to care for him. I was passed from home to home. I often did not have my books, my homework, or a clean change of clothes. I was dropped off early and picked up late, or forgotten, depending on the day.

My fourth-grade teacher was always there for me. She let me stay in and help her. She always waited with me. She was my stability.

As an adult, I reconnected with her and we remained friends until she passed away in 2008. It is amazing how important one caring adult can be in the life of a child.

TEN

Great Ideas from Outstanding Principals

During interviews made for this book, principals were asked to share great ideas they had implemented at school sites. These ideas range from instructional to just plain fun. This chapter offers a compendium of these ideas.

CELEBRATIONS

Our tradition is that the start of each new school year is an incredible celebra-tion. The feelings of renewal and excitement jump-start the new school year.

The first day begins with all staff lining up outside the bus doors like a receiving line. Then we all applaud and cheer for the students as they come off the bus. Balloons, cheerleaders, decorations, and a DJ plays music as the students enter the school for the first time.

All of the students have a picnic lunch with their teachers outside. The day is filled with team-building and icebreaking activities to help the students gain a sense of family, belongingness, and school community.

—Dr. Michael P. Lucas, National Blue Ribbon School Principal,
Pennsylvania

DEALING WITH DIFFICULT BEHAVIOR

I was looking at disciplinary data from recess. I noticed there was a thread of anger running through the referrals. I did some searching and came up with some curriculum ideas.

I brought these kids in when they weren't angry. I did some talking about anger and how it impacts your ability to think. I asked the kids if they thought this was something they would like to work on when they were calm and not worked up. They all liked the idea of reducing anger's impact on their decision-making abilities.

The kids are being very successful this year. It surprised me, because I thought it was such a huge thing in their lives that we wouldn't be able to change it. I was surprised how much change I saw in these kids. . . . I think the relationship we had built was significant. I did not go in with lofty goals. I just thought, "Jeez, I've got to do something."

—Bruce Cannard, National Distinguished Principal, Washington

ENCOURAGEMENT

I have a "twin" I call Bernard Cannard who dresses up and goes in to class-rooms on Fridays. He gives words of encouragement. He gives words of pride and happiness in the students' work. He tells the kids, if they see his twin brother, tell him to take Mom to get her hair cut this afternoon. The little kids totally believe it.

—Bruce Cannard, National Distinguished Principal, Washington

HALLWAY DISPLAYS

Since we want our students to become critical thinkers, we supplement best practices and differentiated classroom instruction with interactive hallway displays throughout the entire school. Student- and teacher-generated verbal and visual puzzles, polls, questions, and interactive activities that flow from the curriculum line our hallways.

—Dr. Jane Koberlein, National Distinguished Principal, Missouri

INSTRUCTION: APPLYING BRAIN RESEARCH EACH DAY

One of our primary teams receives twenty minutes of physical education and twenty minutes of music based on brain research related to exercise and math. Specialists in both areas teach their curriculum, while having students engage

in aerobic movements and reinforcing math concepts. Physical education and music classes are followed by the learning of math. The results have reinforced the research that students do better with the learning of new math skills after aerobic exercise.

—Jan-Marie S. Fernandez, National Distinguished Principal, Virginia

LEARNING ENVIRONMENT

For the past few years, we have been actively building our outdoor environment to provide a learning opportunity for students that stretches beyond the four walls of the classroom. Currently, we have an outdoor castle amphitheater where teachers can teach lessons to entire grade levels and students have a stage where they can demonstrate projects. We also have a fish pond with goldfish, and fountains and gardens where students can grow their own fruits and vegetables and then pick them to eat.

—Stephanie Sullivan, National Distinguished Principal, Kentucky

PARENT INVOLVEMENT: COMPUTER ACCESS

Our goal was to get 70 percent of our parents passwords [on the computer] so they could check grades daily. They did not have computers . . . so I went to a connection of mine and they donated eighty computers. We kept fifty for a computer lab, and gave about thirty away to parents lacking computers at home. The parents then went to the local Walmart and got dial-up Internet access, and now 85 percent of the parents have passwords.

—Jonathan A. Ross, National Distinguished Principal, Pennsylvania

BOARD GAME NIGHT

We have a number of parents that don't speak English and are unlikely to read to their children at night. We wanted them to do something to interact with the children. So we got board games in Spanish, taught the families how to play the games at Board Game Night, and then gave the games to the families at the end of the evening. Maybe the parents can't read to the children, but this is a way they can interact that is better than nothing. We don't want our students just sitting at home watching television, we want them interacting with their parents.

—Theresa Archuleta, National Distinguished Principal, New Mexico

CLASSICAL CAFÉ

Another simple (read: "Free!") way we welcome parents into the school is by having "Classical Café" Fridays during our two lunch periods. We invited parents and relatives to perform on an instrument of their choice, giving two performances to the children as they munch on their lunch.

We have hosted grandpas playing "doo wop" on the saxophone, tickling the ivories, and blasting the harmonica. We've also had roaming violinists, head-banging drummers, coffeehouse bohemians, and guitar-strumming sing-along stepdads. And just to put the icing on the cake, we cover all of our long cafeteria tables with red-and-white checkered tablecloths and pretty 'em up with a mini-vase of flowers in the middle. The kids get a kick out of it, and it also draws teachers and staff into the lunchroom.

—Dr. Christopher Kennedy, National Distinguished Principal,
Rhode Island

LET'S GO FLY A KITE

Our students build kites and as they build, they have to do some forms of measurement. . . . The activity has to do with math. They get to fly their kites, and if their math was right, the kites will fly. It is beautiful. It is something very special to see the parents flying the kites. Everybody comes.

—Cynthia L. Rodriguez, National Blue Ribbon School Principal, Texas

MYSTERY READERS

A key component to becoming an avid reader is being surrounded by adult role models who are committed to and enjoy reading. Our primary level (K–2) has a special "Mystery Reader" program. Parents are invited to sign up as "Mystery Readers of the Week." They choose a favorite children's book or two to read to the class. Many parents bring props or dress up to make their stories come alive. Dads and moms alike take time away from their busy schedules to take part in the program.

—Dr. Jane Koberlein, National Distinguished Principal, Missouri

FAMILY NIGHTS WITH FOOD

The families of any students who have not shown adequate growth in their test data, are not meeting standards, or are in danger of falling further behind are invited to a parent meeting. We first feed the family. Then we tell them what

we are doing in terms of interventions with their child. Then we give them goodie bags of games that are instructional. We bring parents in and teach them how to do these games so they can go home and help their children.

—Jason Cameron, National Blue Ribbon School Principal, Delaware

HELPING STUDENTS OF POVERTY

We have a lot of basic needs not getting met, so we wrote a grant that pays for a family liaison. That person helps with clothing, outreach to families, helps people fill out forms they need to qualify for basic services, and helps them with school supplies. If they are battered women, the liaison helps them to find shelter. The only thing I ask in return is that parents bring their children to school on time.

—Theresa Archuleta, National Distinguished Principal, New Mexico

REWARDS

We are near a military base, so we use dog tag–style rewards on a chain that students and staff can collect. They earn them for all kinds of things. They don't have to be academically strong to get one. We give them for birthdays, random acts of kindness, honor roll, attendance, good grades, and not being in trouble. If they don't get discipline referrals or miss days, they get a red tag and it buys them privileges. Since we have started doing this, our attendance is at 97 percent. Our parents sometimes get mad at us because their kids won't miss school for anything. We found that instead of giving them a bunch of rules, we say, "Hey, if you do this, you get this." It works for us.

We do a transition camp when students are coming to the middle school. We show them their lockers, teachers, how we rotate classes . . . so when the kids come in for the first time it's not as difficult. We have a cookout with the parents. Then our kids are eager to come to school. They are excited.

—Sammy Jackson, National Blue Ribbon School Principal, Oklahoma

STUDENT LEADERSHIP

Our fifth grade students, as leaders of the school, meet our younger students at the front door and then walk them to their classrooms each morning. They create a welcome atmosphere for the younger, more timid children and help their day begin with a smile.

—Dr. Joann Borchetta, National Distinguished Principal, Connecticut

VOLUNTEERS

We have a partnership with our local senior center. Each year we have at least one class that is pen pals with some of our local senior citizens. A pen pal notebook goes back and forth from the student to the senior citizen. This encourages positive relationships with our students and older members of the community. Several times throughout the year they get together and have a party.

—Kay L. Collins, National Distinguished Principal, Colorado

WELLNESS

Our Wellness Team, which is made up of staff and students, encourages all staff and students to eat healthy and be engaged in physical activities. The team provides a variety of before- and after-school activities for both students and staff such as Monday Morning Walking Club, Girls on the Run, Running Club, and intramural basketball teams. Staff teams complete wellness challenges, tracking points for exercise, healthy eating, and weight loss.

—Jan-Marie S. Fernandez, National Distinguished Principal, Virginia

WRITING

We have worked on the six traits of writing. We wanted to highlight the six traits and encourage kids to use them in writing. We created a "tree" in the lobby of our building. Each color of the leaves symbolizes one of those six traits, so if the teacher thought a child had created a good example of one of the six traits, the child could bring a "leaf" up to the office with their name on it and staple it on the wall. Once a week I pick one of the names. It is a beautiful display, in full "bloom."

—Robert J. Slane, National Blue Ribbon School Principal, Wisconsin

IMPLICATIONS FOR ACTION

Borrow ideas from our study participants from across the nation. These are ideas they freely share in the hope of enhancing your work as a principal.

Appendix: Tools for Principals

This appendix provides a number of helpful tools such as checklists, lists of questions, and sample documents for principals to use in improving the academic and learning environments of their schools.

In this appendix you will find:

- A checklist of questions to use during classroom visits when gathering initial information about a school site
- A checklist of questions to assess school-level data work
- A checklist of discussion questions for teachers, in order to structure dialogue and discussion about the need for changes to improve student learning
- A checklist of questions for classroom visits while working to improve the classroom experience of underperforming students
- A checklist of suggestions for an instructional team to identify the most helpful data to assess lower-performing students
- A list of questions that may be part of "courageous conversations" with the adults involved in the lives of lower-performing students, in order to raise awareness of the difficulties these children face
- Steps for writing a letter of reprimand for a teacher or other school employee
- A sample letter of reprimand
- Steps in an employee improvement plan
- A sample employee improvement plan

INITIAL INFORMATION GATHERING: A CHECKLIST FOR CLASSROOM VISITS

The following are just a few of the many possible questions a principal may ask when making initial discoveries of the need for change at a school site. This checklist is for a principal's observation of classroom visits.

- Is the teacher providing solid instruction the first time a concept is taught?
- What are the students in this classroom actively doing?
- How much time does the teacher spend teaching lessons, as opposed to how time much is spent on activities? Is this ratio appropriate?
- Does the teacher effectively model the lesson?
- Does instruction that precedes the students' independent work adequately prepare students to work independently?
- What does the teacher do when students are successful in comprehending a lesson? Are successfully learned concepts reinforced for long-term recall and mastery?
- How does the teacher know when students have grasped a concept? Does he or she check for understanding in effective ways? How does the teacher determine—in a student-by-student fashion—who understood and who did not?
- What does the teacher do when students fail to comprehend a lesson? What interventions are in place for those who do not learn a concept the first time?
- Is the teacher using instructional time effectively and efficiently?
- Are students taught key concepts when their minds are fresh, or is critical instructional time at the beginning of the day lost to administrative tasks that are less important to student learning?

INITIAL INFORMATION GATHERING: A CHECKLIST FOR SCHOOL-LEVEL DATA WORK

The following are questions a principal may ask when making initial discoveries at a school where there is a need for change. This checklist is to be used when a principal is examining student assessment outcomes and data points.

- In what areas are the majority of students making at least one year of progress when they have received one year of instruction?
- What subject areas are strongest for the majority of students? What subjects are the weakest?
- What groups of students are lagging behind others instructionally?

- What groups of students, at what grade levels, have made the most progress in recent years?
- According to data trends, which teachers seem to work best with harder-to-reach students?
- Is there an overall trend at the school to close the achievement gap between ethnic groups?
- How does data compare between genders in age-alike groups?
- How are grade-level groups progressing? For example, did last year's ninth graders make as much or more progress than they made in the prior year?
- What do participation rates and student outcomes reveal about the motivation of students and their attitudes about testing?

INITIAL INFORMATION GATHERING: A CHECKLIST OF DISCUSSION QUESTIONS FOR TEACHERS

The following are questions a principal may ask of teachers, in order to structure dialogue and discussion about the need for changes to improve student learning.

- When you reflect on instruction in your classroom, what is working well?
- What do you find to be challenging or difficult in your classroom?
- What resources do you need to do your job most effectively?
- Which of your students tend to make the most progress? Which students cause you the most concern? Which students appear to be making the least progress? Why do you think this is the case?
- How can I offer you better support as you teach your students? Are there ways I can help you teach more effectively—for example, in a way that helps students grasp a concept the first time you teach it?
- How can I better support you in re-teaching or intervening when students do not understand a lesson or concept?
- In what ways are systems, schedules, or habits at our school—such as the use of public address announcements, the timing of assemblies, the use of the telephone, or any regular interruptions to instructional time—getting in the way of your ability to teach? What changes do we need to make to these systems, schedules, or school habits?

- Do recesses and transitions allow your students to take breaks at appropriate times during the day?

GATHERING INFORMATION ON UNDERPERFORMING STUDENTS: A CHECKLIST FOR CLASSROOM VISITS

The following are questions a principal and instructional team may use for classroom visits while working to improve the classroom experience of underperforming students.

- Does the teacher call on low-achieving students as frequently as other students?
- Are minority students seated equitably with other students throughout the room, or are they seated at the back or in the corners of the classroom?
- Have modifications been made to assist those who do not speak English well? For example, is it an accepted practice in the classroom to seat an English-proficient student near each non-English speaker to help assist with translation as needed?
- Does teaching allow non-native English speakers to grasp grade-level concepts in a way that they can comprehend linguistically? Are modifications made to assist them with issues of English language acquisition?
- Does the teacher spend more time with underperforming students than with other students? Ideally, the teacher should do this if he or she hopes to improve their performance.
- Are other adults available in the classroom to provide assistance to the teacher? If so, are they used to help students to learn, understand, or reinforce the curriculum? Or, by contrast, are they doing less critical work—for example, putting up posters, grading papers, or running copies?
- Are appropriate curricular resources available to meet the needs of underachieving students and take them to the next level of instruction?

GATHERING INFORMATION ON UNDERPERFORMING STUDENTS: A CHECKLIST FOR DATA REVIEW

This list of suggestions is provided to help a principal and instructional team identify important data for assessment of lower-performing students on the school campus. Consider the following sets of data:

- The success of groups of traditionally underperforming students in the classrooms of individual teachers. Also look at the history of each teacher's ability to make a difference with low-achieving students.
- Individual student progress from year to year for students in designated subgroups.
- The progress of low-achieving subgroups of students, versus other subgroups. Ask why some of these groups may be performing less well than others. Make a list of present interventions that are being carried out in the school in light of this data, and attempt to find trends.

Then:

- Consider what the data that has been collected reveals about school-wide efforts to bridge achievement gaps.
- Monitor individual teacher and grade-level efforts in working with students from low-achieving subgroups.
- Look at the progress of individual students who are either markedly improving or notably declining in their performance.

GATHERING INFORMATION ON UNDERPERFORMING STUDENTS: COURAGEOUS CONVERSATIONS

When discussing the difficulties lower-performing students face, these questions may help a principal engage in conversation with teachers, school staff, parents, and other adults who are involved in the lives of the students.

- Does the underperforming student feel successful and comfortable at school, and understand that someone at the school cares about him or her?
- Does this student believe he or she can be successful academically?

- Do the student's peers consider it "cool" to be academically successful?
- In general, do teachers, the principal, counselors, parents, and the surrounding community believe lower-achieving students can be successful?
- Are the adults in a particular student's life—and especially the student's teacher—willing to take steps to bridge the gaps that exist in the child's academic performance?
- School-wide, are teachers, parents, and the surrounding community willing to take steps to improve the academic performance of low-achieving groups of students?
- Who on the school staff and in the community is most passionate about improving the situation of low-achieving students? Are these adults ready and willing to help correct problems in the lives of children?
- Do parents of at-risk, poor, minority, non-native English-speaking, or special education students feel welcome on the school campus? Do they understand the language and jargon of the school setting? Do these parents know or understand how they can best help their child learn in this school setting?
- What life challenges face the school's low-performing students? Are there meaningful ways the school can help improve such situations or help students overcome some of the burdens they may face at home or in the community?

STEPS IN A LETTER OF REPRIMAND

Here are steps that a principal may follow when writing a letter of reprimand for a teacher or other school employee:

1. Describe the problem that has been observed with regard to the teacher or employee's work performance. Include in this statement any rule, policy, or law the employee has violated.
2. Explain the impact of this behavior on others, especially its effect on students, other school staff, school safety, and parent perceptions.
3. Spell out in detail any changes in employee behavior and/or work performance that the principal expects to see in the future.

4. Explain what form of support will be offered in order to help the teacher or employee to improve his or her work performance.
5. Provide a timeline by which expected changes are to take place and provide a date on which the principal will revisit this issue with the employee to check for improvement.

SAMPLE LETTER OF REPRIMAND

This sample letter is provided as a model for principals to use when it becomes necessary to record in writing an official reprimand of a teacher or other employee.

To: Ms. Jane Doe
From: Principal Smith
Date:
Re: Letter of Reprimand

On April 10, I walked by your classroom at 10 a.m. and found your class unattended. The students were running around the room and playing. Some students were practicing karate moves by play-fighting and kicking one another. I found you next door, talking with Mr. Hernandez about the party on Friday.

Similar incidents occurred previously on March 8 and again on March 24. On both prior occasions I spoke with you about the incident and asked you to appropriately supervise your students. On March 24, I issued a written letter of reprimand to you regarding the incident.

When you leave your class unattended, it affects the students in your class and threatens the safety of your students, because no adult is present to ensure that they do not cause harm to themselves or others.

Effective immediately, you are to maintain close supervision of your class when the students are under your care. Specifically, you are to remain in the same room with your students or you are to remain within twenty feet of your students and maintain full visual contact with students when they are in your care.

In order to assist you in better understanding appropriate supervision of students, I am requiring you to watch a video series on effective strategies for appropriate student supervision in the classroom setting. Also, I have arranged for you to observe in Mrs. Brown's class, and then talk with her about her strategies for providing appropriate oversight of her class. I will provide release time for this classroom visit.

Finally, when we meet next, I will talk with you about these two experiences and will answer any questions that may arise for you as a result of watching the video series and observing in Mrs. Brown's class.

An immediate improvement in how you supervise your students is expected. I plan to revisit this issue with you in person on May 3 at 2 p.m. Please come to my office for this meeting. At that time, I anticipate you will have taken the above-mentioned steps. It is my expectation that from this date forward, appropriate supervision will no longer be an issue in your classroom.

Sincerely,
Principal Smith

STEPS IN AN EMPLOYEE IMPROVEMENT PLAN

A principal may take the following steps to create and write an improvement plan for a teacher or other school employee who has received a letter of reprimand.

1. Outline the problem. Explain what the employee is doing that is unsatisfactory.
2. Tell how the unsatisfactory behavior or inappropriate actions negatively impact others, spelling out the negative effects for students in particular, but also including negative effects for other school staff, parents, and the school environment in general.
3. List the improvements the principal wishes to see in the performance of the employee.
4. This step makes an improvement plan different from a letter of reprimand: Outline a long-term plan for the next three to nine months, describing improvements that the teacher or employee is expected to carry out. In contrast with the letter of reprimand's short-term expectations, the improvement plan looks for long-term improvement over a period of weeks or months. For deficits that are potentially easier to fix, such as timeliness, the principal may suggest a three-month window in which to solve the problem. If, however, the issue is one of preparedness for the profession, such as teaching effectively, the window of time for the employee should be much longer, such as nine months or a year, to allow time for growth and improvement. Tell the employee the timeline

by which expected changes are to be made. Give a date on which the principal and the employee will revisit the issue.

SAMPLE IMPROVEMENT PLAN

This sample improvement plan may provide ideas as principals create and write improvement plans for teachers or school employees under reprimand.

Principal Smith
Washington School
100 Washington Way
Union City, Texas

(Date)

Ms. Mary Jones
200 Main Street
Union City, Texas

Re Improvement Plan

Dear Ms. Jones,

The following improvement plan is intended to correct an issue that has become a problem for your students. It is anticipated you will follow this plan to improve your teaching performance.

As we have discussed, when you use a loud, abrasive tone of voice with your students, they perceive that you are angry with them. This tone of voice pervades your teaching, and frightens your students.

Children who are afraid do not learn as effectively as they could. They also go home and tell their parents that their teacher is yelling at them. Parents have complained about this behavior, and some want to take their children out of your class.

Effective immediately and from now on, you are directed to speak in an appropriate voice with your students. You must use a softer, gentler tone of voice with your kindergarteners.

I realize that changing the tone of voice you use in teaching will take work. In order to assist you, I am providing the following support mechanisms:

1. You will receive a decibel meter. This meter flashes red when the decibels of the speaker or classroom exceed a given level. Use this as a guide for the loudness of your voice.

2. Our speech teacher will work with you one-on-one on a weekly basis, and she will make a weekly visit to your classroom to help you learn to monitor your tone of voice.

3. I will meet with you once a month to talk about your perceptions of improvement of this issue, the feedback I have received from parents, and my observations of changes made in the tone you use with students in your classroom.

On May 15, we will revisit this issue. If you are unable to correct the tone of voice you are using with your kindergarteners, you may be reassigned to another grade level. We will discuss this possibility further when we meet at the end of this improvement period.

Sincerely,
Principal Smith

Book Recommendations from Blue Ribbon School and Distinguished Principals

The following list of recommended books was compiled from suggestions submitted by study participants. These titles, listed by category, will be helpful to a principal who is developing a set of resources for professional practice: assessment and use of data, brain research, instruction, response to intervention, special populations, books specifically for principals, and leadership and productivity.

ASSESSMENT AND USE OF DATA

Bernhardt, Victoria L. (2004). *Data Analysis* (second edition). Larchmont, NY: Eye on Education.

O'Connor, Ken. (2010). *A Repair Kit for Grading: Fifteen Fixes for Broken Grades* (second edition). Columbus, OH: Allyn and Bacon.

Stiggins, Richard J., Judith A. Arter, Jan Chappuis, and Stephen Chappuis. (2009). *Classroom Assessment for Student Learning: Doing It Right—Using It Well*. Columbus, OH: Allyn and Bacon.

BRAIN RESEARCH

Brown, Jeffrey, and Mark J. Fenske, with Liz Neporent. (2011). *The Winner's Brain: Eight Strategies Great Minds Use to Achieve Success*. Cambridge, MA: Da Capo Press.

Medina, John. (2009). *Brain Rules: Twelve Principles for Surviving and Thriving at Work, Home, and School* (reprint edition). Seattle, WA: Pear Press.

Ratey, John J., with Eric Hagerman. (2008). *Spark: The Revolutionary New Science of Exercise and the Brain*. New York: Little, Brown, and Company.

Siegel, Daniel J. (2007). *The Mindful Brain: Reflection and Attunement in the Cultivation of Well-Being*. New York: W.W. Norton & Company, Inc.

Souza, David A. (2006). *How the Brain Learns* (third edition). Thousand Oaks, CA: Corwin Press.

INSTRUCTION

Allen, Patrick A. (2009). *Conferring: The Keystone of Reader's Workshop*. Portland, ME: Stenhouse Publishers.

Bellanca, James, and Ron Brandt. (2010). *21st Century Skills: Rethinking How Students Learn*. Bloomington, IN: Solution Tree Press.

Buckner, Aimee, and Ralph Fletcher. (2005). *Notebook Know-How: Strategies for the Writer's Notebook*. Portland, ME: Stenhouse Publishers.

Conzemius, Anne, and Jan O'Neill. (2005). *The Power of SMART Goals: Using Goals to Improve Student Learning*. Bloomington, IN: Solution Tree Press.

Dehaene, Stanislas. (1997). *The Number Sense: How the Mind Creates Mathematics* (revised and updated edition 2011). New York: Oxford University Press.

Diller, Debbie (2008). *Spaces and Places: Designing Classrooms for Literacy*. Portland, ME: Stenhouse Publishers.

Dorfman, Lynne R. (2009). *Nonfiction Mentor Texts: Teaching Informational Writing through Children's Literature, K–8*. Portland, ME: Stenhouse Publishers.

DuFour, Rebecca, Robert Eaker, Gayle Karhanek, and Richard DuFour. (2004). *Whatever It Takes—How Professional Learning Communities Respond When Kids Don't Learn*. Bloomington, IN: Solution Tree Press.

Gallagher, Kelly. (2009). *Readicide: How Schools Are Killing Reading and What You Can Do About It*. Portland, ME: Stenhouse Publishers.

Gear, Adrienne. (2008). *Nonfiction Reading Power: Teaching Students How to Think While They Read All Kinds of Information*. Markham, Ontario: Pembroke Publishers.

Hale, Elizabeth (2008). *Crafting Writers, K–6*. Portland, ME: Stenhouse Publishers.

Harvey, Stephanie. (1998). *Nonfiction Matters: Reading, Writing, and Research in Grades 3–8*. Portland, ME: Stenhouse Publishers.

Heard, Georgia. (2009). *A Place for Wonder: Reading and Writing Nonfiction in the Primary Grades*. Portland, ME: Stenhouse Publishers.

Johnson, Pat. (2010). *Catching Readers Before They Fall: Supporting Readers Who Struggle, K–4*. Portland, ME: Stenhouse Publishers.

Jones, Fredric H., Patrick Jones, Fred Jones, and Jo Lynn. (2007). *Fred Jones Tools for Teaching: Discipline, Instruction, Motivation*. Santa Cruz, CA: Fredric H. Jones & Associates, Inc.

Keene, Ellin Oliver. (2008). *To Understand: New Horizons in Reading Comprehension*. Portsmouth, NH: Heinemann.

Kempton, Susan L. (2007). The *Literate Kindergarten: Where Wonder and Discovery Thrive*. Portsmouth, NH: Heinemann.

Lemov, Doug. (2010). *Teach Like a Champion: Forty-Nine Techniques that Put Students on the Path to College*. San Francisco: Jossey-Bass.

Marzano, Robert J., Debra J. Pickering, and Jane E. Pollock. (2001). *Classroom Instruction That Works: Research-Based Strategies for Increasing Student Achievement*. Alexandria, VA: Association for Supervision and Curriculum Development.

McCain, Ted. (2005). *Teaching for Tomorrow: Teaching Content and Problem-Solving Skills*. Thousand Oaks, CA: Corwin Press.

McGregor, Tanny. (2007). *Comprehension Connections: Bridges to Strategic Reading*. Portsmouth, NH: Heinemann.

Miller, Debbie. (2002). *Reading with Meaning*. Portland, ME: Stenhouse Publishers.

Miller, Donalyn. (2009). *The Book Whisperer: Awakening the Inner Reader in Every Child.* San Francisco: Jossey-Bass.

Pollock, Jane E. (2007). *Improving Student Learning One Teacher at a Time.* Alexandria, VA: Association for Supervision and Curriculum Development.

Schmoker, Michael J. (2006). *Results Now: How We Can Achieve Unprecedented Improvements in Teaching and Learning.* Alexandria, VA: Association for Supervision and Curriculum Development.

Tovani, Cris. (2000). *I Read It, But I Don't Get It: Comprehension Strategies for Adolescent Readers.* Portland, ME: Stenhouse Publishers.

Willingham, Daniel T. (2010). *Why Don't Students Like School: A Cognitive Scientist Answers Questions about How the Mind Works and What It Means for the Classroom.* San Francisco: Jossey-Bass.

Wood Ray, Katie. (1999). *Wondrous Words: Writers and Writing in the Elementary Classroom.* Urbana, IL: National Council of Teachers of English.

Zimmermann, Susan, and Chryse Hutchins. (2003). *Seven Keys to Comprehension: How to Help Your Kids Read It and Get It!* New York: Three Rivers Press.

RESPONSE TO INTERVENTION

Bender, William N., and Cara F. Shores (Eds.). (2007). *Response to Intervention: A Practical Guide for Every Teacher.* Thousand Oaks, CA: Corwin Press.

Brown-Chidsey, Rachel, and Mark W. Steege. (2010). *Response to Intervention: Principles and Strategies for Effective Practice* (second edition). New York: The Guilford Press.

Buffum, Austin, Chris Weber, and Mike Mattos. (2008). *Pyramid Response to Intervention: RTI, Professional Learning Communities, and How to Respond When Kids Don't Learn.* Bloomington, IN: Solution Tree Press.

Howard, Mary and Linda Hoyt. (2009). *RTI from All Sides: What Every Teacher Needs to Know.* Portsmouth, NH: Heinemann.

Quinn, Pat. (2010). *Ultimate RTI: Everything a Teacher Needs to Know to Implement RTI* (expanded second edition). Slinger, WI: Ideas Unlimited Seminars.

SPECIAL POPULATIONS

Beegle, Donna M. (2007). *See Poverty . . . Be the Difference!* Tigard, OR: Communication Across Barriers.

Darling-Hammond, Linda. (2010). *The Flat World and Education: How America's Commitment to Equity Will Determine Our Future.* New York: Teachers College Press.

Shaywitz, Sally E. (2005). *Overcoming Dyslexia: A New and Complete Science-Based Program for Reading Problems at Any Level.* New York: Vintage.

Weinfeld, Rich, Sue Jeweler, Linda Barnes-Robinson, and Becky Roffman Shevitz. (2006). *Smart Kids with Learning Difficulties: Overcoming Obstacles and Realizing Potential.* Waco, TX: Prufrock Press, Inc.

Whitaker, Todd. (2003). *What Great Teachers Do Differently: Fourteen Things That Matter Most.* Larchmont, NY: Eye on Education.

SPECIFICALLY FOR PRINCIPALS

Black, John A. (2002). *What They Don't Tell You in Schools of Education about School Administration*. Lanham, MD: Scarecrow Press.

Deal, Terrence E. (2009). *Shaping School Culture: Pitfalls, Paradoxes, and Promises* (second edition). San Francisco: Jossey-Bass.

Goodlad, John I. (2004). *A Place Called School: Twentieth Anniversary Edition*. New York: McGraw-Hill.

Gordon, Gary. (2006). *Building Engaged Schools: Getting the Most Out of America's Classrooms*. New York: Gallup Press.

Gray, Susan Penny, and William A. Streshly. (2008). *From Good Schools to Great Schools: What Their Principals Do Well*. Thousand Oaks, CA: Corwin Press.

Krzyzewski, Mike, with Donald T. Phillips. (2001). *Leading with the Heart: Coach K's Successful Strategies for Basketball, Business, and Life*. New York: Warner Business Books.

McEwan-Adkins, Elaine K. (2001). *Ten Traits of Highly Effective Teachers: How to Hire, Coach, and Mentor Successful Teachers*. Thousand Oaks, CA: Corwin Press.

Reeves, D. B. (2006). *The Learning Leader: How to Focus School Improvement for Better Results*. Alexandria, VA: Association for Supervision and Curriculum Development.

Sergiovanni, Thomas J. (2008). *The Principalship: A Reflective Practice Perspective*. Bloomington, IN: Solution Tree Press.

Whitaker, Todd. (2002). *What Great Principals Do Differently: Fifteen Things That Matter Most*. Larchmont, NY: Eye on Education.

LEADERSHIP AND PRODUCTIVITY

Allen, David. (2002). *Getting Things Done: The Art of Stress-Free Productivity*. New York: Penguin Books.

Belsky, Scott. (2010). *Making Ideas Happen: Overcoming the Obstacles between Vision and Reality*. New York: Portfolio Penguin.

Brady, Chris, and Orrin Woodward. (2005) *Launching a Leadership Revolution: Mastering the Five Levels of Influence*. New York: Business Plus.

Carnegie, Dale. (1936). *How to Win Friends and Influence People* (hardcover revised edition 2009). New York: Simon and Schuster.

Collins, J. (2001). *Good to Great*. New York: Harper Business.

Covey, Stephen R. (2004). *The Seven Habits of Highly Effective People* (revised edition). New York: Free Press.

Frick, Don M., and Larry C. Spears. (1996). *On Becoming a Servant Leader: The Private Writings of Robert K. Greenleaf*. San Francisco: Jossey-Bass.

Gordon, Jon. (2007). *The Energy Bus: Ten Rules to Fuel Your Life, Work, and Team with Positive Energy*. Hoboken, NJ: John Wiley and Sons.

Heath, Chip, and Dan Heath. (2010). *Switch: How to Change Things When Change Is Hard*. New York: Broadway Books.

Littky, Dennis, and Samantha Grabelle. (2004). *The Big Picture: Education Is Everyone's Business.* Alexandria, VA: Association for Supervision and Curriculum Development.

Pink, Daniel H. (2009). *Drive: The Surprising Truth about What Motivates Us.* New York: Riverhead Books.

List of Study Participants

Theresa Archuleta, New Mexico, National Distinguished Principal*
Dr. Angel J. Barrett, California, National Distinguished Principal
Janice Barton, Mississippi, National Blue Ribbon School Principal**
Sister Marie Blanchette, Tennessee, National Blue Ribbon School Principal
Dr. Joann Borchetta, Connecticut, National Distinguished Principal
John-Mark Cain, Mississippi, National Blue Ribbon School Principal
Jason Cameron, Delaware, National Blue Ribbon School Principal
Bruce Cannard, Washington, National Distinguished Principal
Kay L. Collins, Colorado, National Distinguished Principal
W. Fred Crawford, South Carolina, National Blue Ribbon School Principal
Budd A. Dingwall, North Carolina, National Distinguished Principal
Andrew M. Doell, New York, National Blue Ribbon School Principal
Jan-Marie S. Fernandez, Virginia, National Distinguished Principal
Jill Flanders, Massachusetts, National Distinguished Principal
Marty French, South Carolina, National Blue Ribbon School Principal
Michael E. Friel, Lebanon, National Distinguished Principal
Anne Gold, Maryland, National Distinguished Principal
Karen Grass, Virginia, National Blue Ribbon School Principal
Dr. Jolie D. Hardin, Georgia, National Distinguished Principal
Valerie L. Hatcher, California, National Blue Ribbon School Principal
John Haynal, Nevada, National Blue Ribbon School Principal
Peter Heinze, Texas, National Blue Ribbon School Principal
Juliann DePalma Hesed, Missouri, National Blue Ribbon School Principal
Jeff Hornby, Montana, National Blue Ribbon School Principal
Brian M. Hull, Virginia, National Distinguished Principal
Terry L. Hurlburt, Iowa, National Distinguished Principal
Dr. Michael Israel, New York, National Blue Ribbon School Principal
Sammy Jackson, Oklahoma, National Blue Ribbon School Principal
Lucille Keaton, Nevada, National Distinguished Principal

Dr. Christopher Kennedy, Rhode Island, National Distinguished Principal

Dr. Jane Koberlein, Missouri, National Distinguished Principal

Carol Krichbaum, Virginia, National Blue Ribbon School Principal

Dr. Michael P. Lucas, Pennsylvania, National Blue Ribbon School Principal

Patricia Mary Salleh Matta, Kenya, National Distinguished Principal

Dr. Dana McCauley, Maryland, National Distinguished Principal

Jacquelyn Meyer, Idaho, National Distinguished Principal

Larry Nauta, Alaska, National Blue Ribbon School Principal

Sanford E. Nelson, Minnesota, National Distinguished Principal

Nancy A. Nettik, Rhode Island, National Distinguished Principal

Rhonda M. Parmer, Texas, National Distinguished Principal

Andrew Polsky, California, National Blue Ribbon School Principal

Bruce E. Reynolds, Oregon, National Distinguished Principal

Cynthia L. Rodriguez, Texas, National Blue Ribbon School Principal

Wayne C. Roellich, Washington, National Blue Ribbon School Principal

Jonathan A. Ross, Pennsylvania, National Distinguished Principal

Richard W. Salo, Michigan, National Distinguished Principal

Dr. Paul M. Schley, Wisconsin, National Blue Ribbon School Principal

Robert J. Slane, Wisconsin, National Blue Ribbon School Principal

Stephanie Sullivan, Kentucky, National Distinguished Principal

Kelly Wilmore, Virginia, National Blue Ribbon School Principal

Beth M. York, Tennessee, National Blue Ribbon School Principal

*National Distinguished Principal: The National Association of Elementary School Principals (NAESP) honors one principal per state per year for outstanding leadership. "Established in 1984 by NAESP in cooperation with the U.S. Department of Education, the program recognizes public and private school principals who make superior contributions to their schools and communities. The distinguished principals are selected by NAESP state affiliates, including the District of Columbia, and by committees representing private and overseas schools" (www.naesp.org).

**National Blue Ribbon School Principal: The U.S. Department of Education designates schools in grades K–12, both public and private, as Blue Ribbon Schools for demonstrating success either by being in the top 10

percent of all districts in the state or by having impressive gains in student achievement, with no less than 40 percent of the student population having come from disadvantaged homes.

About the Author

Linda K. Wagner, EdD, has been a superintendent in California schools for nine years. She is a credentialed bilingual teacher and administrator with over twenty-four years of experience in the field of education.

Dr. Wagner was named 2009 Superintendent of the Year for the Association of California School Administrators, Region 15. She earned her master's degree in education administration and her doctorate in educational leadership at the University of La Verne in La Verne, California.

Wagner is the author of *The Savvy Superintendent: Leading Instruction to the Top of the Class*, a study of the advice, stories, and experiences of top school superintendents from across the nation, published in 2010 in partnership with the American Association of School Administrators (AASA) and Rowman & Littlefield Education.

Other Titles of Interest by Rowman & Littlefield Education

The Principal as School Manager, Third Edition
William L. Sharp and James K. Walter

American Schools: The Art of Creating a Democratic Learning Community
Sam Chaltain

Passing the Leadership Test: Strategies for Success on the Leadership Licensure Exam, Second Edition
Leslie Jones and Eugene Kennedy

Collaborative School Leadership: Practical Strategies for Principals
Ron Nash and Kathleen Hwang

Total Leaders 2.0: Leading in the Age of Empowerment
Charles J. Schwahn and William G. Spady

Preparing to Be Next in Line: A Guide to the Principalship
Kevin A. Gorman

Stepping into Administration: How to Succeed in Making the Move
Thomas A. Kersten